INSTRUCTOR'S MANUAL AND TEST BANK
TO ACCOMPANY

VOCABULARY BASICS
and
GROUNDWORK FOR A
BETTER VOCABULARY, 2/e

Beth Johnson

Carole Mohr

Janet M. Goldstein

TOWNSEND PRESS   Marlton, NJ 08053

THE TOWNSEND PRESS VOCABULARY SERIES

VOCABULARY BASICS (reading level 4–6)
GROUNDWORK FOR A BETTER VOCABULARY, 2/e (reading level 5–8)
BUILDING VOCABULARY SKILLS, 2/e (reading level 7–9)
IMPROVING VOCABULARY SKILLS, 2/e (reading level 9–11)
ADVANCING VOCABULARY SKILLS, 2/e (reading level 11–13)
BUILDING VOCABULARY SKILLS, SHORT VERSION, 2/e*
IMPROVING VOCABULARY SKILLS, SHORT VERSION, 2/e*
ADVANCING VOCABULARY SKILLS, SHORT VERSION, 2/e*

*The short versions of the three books are limited to 200 words, in contrast
to the 260 words and 40 word parts in each of the long versions. For some
students and classes, the short versions of the books will provide an easier,
more manageable approach to vocabulary development.

Copyright © 1998 by Townsend Press, Inc.
Printed in the United States of America
ISBN 0-944210-43-0
9 8 7 6 5 4 3 2 1

Send book orders to:
Townsend Press
1038 Industrial Drive
West Berlin, New Jersey 08091

For even faster service, call us at our toll-free number:
1-800-772-6410

Or fax your request to:
1-609-753-0649

Instructor's Manual and Test Bank to Accompany
VOCABULARY BASICS
GROUNDWORK FOR A BETTER VOCABULARY, 2/e

ISBN: 0-944210-43-0

Contents

Introduction

BRIEF GUIDELINES FOR USING THE VOCABULARY BOOKS

1. Make sure that the book you are using is at the right instructional level for your students. The two most basic books in the Townsend Press vocabulary series have the following recommended reading levels:

    VOCABULARY BASICS: reading level 4–6

    GROUNDWORK FOR A BETTER VOCABULARY: reading level 5–8

    Ideally, most of your students should have a sense of some of the words in the book you choose. The words may be part of their listening vocabulary if not their sight vocabulary: they will recognize the words upon hearing them, even though they may not recognize the words simply by seeing them in print. As students work through the chapters in the book, they can then strengthen their knowledge of the words they already know, as well as master the words they're only half sure of, or don't know at all.

2. Don't feel you must cover every single chapter in a book. Each book is packed with activities—enough so that students can work on some at home and cover others with you in class. The activities are necessary, for the simple truth is that the more students work with words, the better they will understand them. *It is better to cover fewer words more thoroughly than to try to cover too many too lightly.*

3. The "Adding Words to a Reading" passages in *Vocabulary Basics* and the "Final Check" passages in *Groundwork for a Better Vocabulary* pose a more difficult challenge for students than the sentence-level activities that precede them. To handle the paragraphs, students must have successfully completed the earlier activities. These passages are an excellent opportunity for students to deepen their knowledge of the words in the chapter.

    Because the passages are such a challenge, as well as an opportunity to solidify learning, we recommend that you not use them as mastery tests. Instead, we use the appropriate mastery tests in this test bank.

4. The final activity in each chapter of *Vocabulary Basics* and the final two activities in each chapter of *Groundwork for a Better Vocabulary* ask students to talk or write about the words they have just learned. Such activities increase the likelihood that the words will become part of students' permanent vocabulary.

    To further encourage this "ownership" of the new words, we suggest taking class time to do these activities. Doing so ensures that help is available immediately for students as they work to apply the words they have learned.

5. Pretests are available for each chapter and unit in the books. The pretests start on page 13. You have permission to make unlimited copies of these pretests (and the other materials here, including the mastery tests) if you are currently using one of the vocabulary books in a course. The pretests can be used at the start of a unit, and the posttests at the end of a unit, as an accurate way to measure vocabulary progress and mastery.

A SUGGESTED INSTRUCTIONAL APPROACH

Here is a suggested classroom approach that we think will maintain interest and keep students active in learning the words. You will notice that at several instances the suggestions we offer for *Vocabulary Basics* and *Groundwork for a Better Vocabulary* are not the same. This distinction reflects the different activities and instructional levels of these two books.

First of all, have students work through the introductory section of the book called "To the Student" (beginning on page 1). Don't teach it; have them *read* it (or read it with them), follow the directions, and insert all the answers needed. Then spend a few minutes reviewing their answers and checking their understanding of the material.

Next, give students the pretest for the unit you will be covering. (Such pretests start on pages 21 and 89 of this IM.) Explain that at the end of the unit, they will be given a posttest on the same words, so you and they will be able to measure what they have learned. (Pretests for the entire book are also available—see pages 13 and 81 of this IM—at your option.) Then proceed as follows:

1. Preview each of the words in a chapter by printing the words, one at a time, on the board. Ask students if they can pronounce each word. As needed, write some of the pronunciations on the board. You may also want to use, or ask students to use, some of the words in a sentence. And it's OK to ask for or to give short meanings of some of the words. Don't go into a lot of detail, but make this a good general introduction to the words.

2. Then, based on the verbal preview, ask students to turn to the first page of the chapter. Put students in groups of two or three. (It is hard to overstate the value that small group work can have: if managed successfully, it uses peer pressure to keep everyone involved in the work of the class.) Explain, "Here's what I want you to do. One of you read the first word and the two sentences that contain the word. Make sure the word is being pronounced correctly. Always help each other out with the pronunciation. Then think about the context—the rest of the sentence—very carefully. The context will give you very strong clues as to what the word means. Your ability to use the context surrounding an unfamiliar word is an excellent way to deal with any word you don't know. Then I'd like all of you to see if you can pick out the right meaning from the three answer choices that follow that first word.

    "After you do that, have someone else in your group pronounce the second word and read the two sentences for that word. Then work together again and pick out the right answer choice. And so on, until you've done all the words in this first section. Look up at me when you've done all the words."

3. Of course, not every group will finish the words at exactly the same time. We suggest you take a middle-ground approach to the challenging fact that every group will move at a different speed. When a couple of the groups are finished (and starting to get restless), and others are still working, say, "OK—even if you're not quite finished yet, we're going to go over the words as a class. Somebody please volunteer to pronounce the first word and give us its meaning."

4. After reviewing the pronunciations and meanings of the words, have your students complete the "Matching Words with Meanings" activity on the second page of the

chapter. Say, "Now, that you have figured out what the words mean in sentences, I'd like to see if you can figure out each word's definition." Then you can read the first definition in the matching section and see if any students can figure out which word is the right answer. If students have trouble, you can review the meanings they identified in the previous activity. In this way, you can move through all the words in the chapter.

Only after all students have the proper definitions selected in this section should you move them into the rest of the chapter.

5. In the suggestions we give below for the rest of the chapter, we continue to suggest that students work in groups. However, depending upon the skills and needs of your students, you may wish to have them work independently instead.

For instructors using _Vocabulary Basics:_

Say, "Now I want you to work as a group to complete the next three activities: 'Adding One Word to an Item,' 'Adding Two Words to an Item,' and 'Showing You Understand the Words.' Again, you want to practice looking at context very carefully. Context will give you the clues you need to figure out the meanings of words and answer the items correctly."

For instructors using _Groundwork for a Better Vocabulary:_

Say, "Now I want you to work as a group to complete the next five activities: 'Check 1,' 'Check 2,' 'Related Words,' 'Word Work,' and 'Word Parts.' Again, you want to practice looking at context very carefully. Context will give the clues you need to figure out the meanings of words and answer the items correctly."

6. When several groups are finished, say, "OK, not everyone is quite finished, but we're going to go over the activities you've been working on. Will someone volunteer to read me the first sentence and insert the word needed?" Then go through each of the activities, item by item, answering any questions and clarifying any problems along the way. Certain activities, particularly "Showing You Understand the Words" in _Vocabulary Basics_ and "Word Work" in _Groundwork for a Better Vocabulary,_ are playful and will make this time enjoyable.

7. Next, for the paragraph-completion activities, called "Adding Words to a Reading" in _Vocabulary Basics_ and "Final Check" in _Groundwork for a Better Vocabulary,_ say, "The next activity here is very challenging. Why don't you all work on this individually. Read over the passage once. Then go back and start reading more carefully and slowly and try to put in some of the words. Getting in some of the words will help you do the rest. Then go back a third time to get the remaining words. Remember to pay close attention to the context to figure out the meaning of a word."

8. When about half the people are done, say, "All right—let's review the passage. Would someone read the first couple of sentences and insert the missing words?" Then proceed through the words in each paragraph, helping along the way as needed. In this way students benefit from reading the words, as well as seeing and hearing how the words can be used in a written passage.

9. After your students have completed the paragraphs, assign the final exercises in the chapters as review activities. Here are ways to approach these activities:

For instructors using *Vocabulary Basics:*

"Using the Words When Writing and Talking" is an excellent activity for reinforcing the words students have learned. Depending upon the needs of your students, you can assign it either as a group activity or as an individual assignment.

When you present this section, say, "One way to make sure you don't forget the words you have learned is to use them when you speak or write. See if you can finish each of the partial sentences in the activity. As you come up with answers, write them in the space provided." When most students appear to be finished, say, "Now we are going to see which answers you came up with." Then simply go around the room, having students or a member from each group say the sentence with their answers added. Since answers will vary and some may be funny, this should be a lively classroom activity.

For instructors using *Groundwork for a Better Vocabulary:*

"Questions for Discussion" and "Ideas for Writing" can be used as final reinforcement activities in mastering the words in a chapter. We suggest assigning the "Questions for Discussion" as a group activity. Put students into groups of two to three students and say, "One way to make sure you don't forget the words you have learned is to use them when you speak. I want each of you to read each item and briefly talk about it with your group, using the boldface vocabulary word in your discussion. Make sure everyone in your group gets a chance to answer each item and use each word."

Then, when you sense that students are finished, you can assign them the "Ideas for Writing" activity. This works best as an individual assignment or homework activity. However, if you already have a writing component in your class, you could use this as an extra-credit assignment. Say, "Another way to make the words stick in your memory is to use them in your writing. Write short papers—no more than a paragraph or two—using the words provided."

10. After students have completed all the chapter activities, ask them to review and study the words at home in preparation for a mastery test. At the start of the next class, say, "Spend about two minutes reviewing the words. I'll then pass out a mastery test. I will grade this test, so do your best to remember the words." (Knowing that a grade will be involved always provides students with an extra boost of incentive.)

AN ALTERNATIVE INSTRUCTIONAL APPROACH

An alternative instructional approach is to proceed as described above for steps 1 to 5. Then, instead of having students work in small groups, ask them to work individually on the additional activities. After they are finished, have them come individually to your desk so that you can quickly check their answers, clarify any confusions, and move them on to the paragraph completion activities ("Adding Words to a Reading" in *Vocabulary Basics* and "Final Check" in *Groundwork for a Better Vocabulary).* In this individualized scenario, everyone is working at his or her own pace, and you are working at a very steady pace. When students finish filling in the words in the paragraphs, you can either have them work with people who are not done, move into the speaking and writing activities, or get a head start on another chapter that you plan to assign for homework.

ADDITIONAL ACTIVITIES

Let us repeat a point stated earlier: the more students work with words, the more they can learn. Here are other activities you can use, in addition to the many in the book. Choose whichever combination of activities goes best with your teaching style and the learning styles of your students.

1. **Word cards.** Students can use 3 × 5 or 4 × 6 index cards to create a bank of words. Word cards can help students master words in the book; the cards are also a helpful tool for learning unknown words that students come across in reading. Students simply jot down an unfamiliar word on the front of the card. Then, when they have finished their reading, they can complete the front and back of a card. Here is a suggested format:

Front of card

p. 27, VB	Adjective
precious	
Synonym—valuable	*Antonym—worthless*

Back of card

1) Worth a lot, having great value

2) The painting is so <u>precious</u> that the museum will never sell it .

3) My husband's most <u>precious</u> possession is his grandfather's watch.

5

Note that the front of the card has the target word, the page number and source where the word can be located, the part of speech, a synonym, and an antonym. The back of the card has three entries: 1) the definition, based on the way the word is used in context; 2) a phrase or sentence showing the word in context (this can be taken from the source where the student has come upon the word); and 3) a student-created sentence which shows an understanding of the word. Students can use this same format when they encounter unfamiliar words in their textbooks and other reading.

2. **Identifying words.** Present lists of words written as pronunciations and ask students to identify the words. For example, here are pronunciations of several words in Unit One of *Groundwork for a Better Vocabulary*:

soo′tə-bəl   _____(suitable)_____
frăj′əl   _____(fragile)_____
skârs   _____(scarce)_____

And here are pronunciations of several words in Unit One of *Vocabulary Basics:*

kyoor-ee-uhss   _____(curious)_____
ii-**den**-tuh-fii   _____(identify)_____
klaym   _____(claim)_____

3. **Imaging.** The use of imagery as a way of remembering vocabulary words has been researched rather extensively. Results typically indicate that students who are trained to use imagery techniques—or in simple terms, told to "form pictures in their minds"—remember the meanings of words better than those who do not employ such techniques.

Here's an example: Think of a little boy who is taken to his mother just after being rescued from a burning building. His mother thought he was dead. The boy wears a T-shirt with the letters E - M - B -R - A -C - E written on it. When the mother sees her son, she hugs him tightly.

We suggest taking five or ten minutes every once in a while to have students get a piece of paper and write up their images—the more vivid the better—for remembering a given word in a chapter. Then ask students to hand in the paper (signing their names to the paper is optional). Quickly flip through the papers, reading the most effective ones aloud to the class.

4. **Generating sentences.** Have students generate their own sentences using the words, or as a more advanced activity, have them write a story using five of the words. (You may want to have a department assistant working with you for these activities, which require individual checking and detailed feedback.)

SUGGESTED SYLLABI

Suggested Syllabus for Using the Book as a Core Text

Since each book consists of five units, each containing five *(GBV)* or six *(VB)* chapters packed with activities, it can easily serve as a core text for a vocabulary course—especially when supplemented by the test bank and the computer disks. In a fifteen-week class that meets three hours a week, you can cover two lessons in two class hours. The third class hour can be used for the unit tests that close each of the five units in each book, as well as for the pretests, posttests, and mastery tests.

We recommend strongly that students be encouraged to do a lot of reading at the same time that they are learning vocabulary words. For remedial and developmental students, widespread reading, in addition to continuing, intensive work on vocabulary, is the best way to develop vocabulary skills.

Suggested Syllabus for Using the Book as a Supplement in a Reading Course

In many courses, the vocabulary book will serve as a supplementary text. In such cases, and assuming a fifteen-week semester with three hours of class a week, either of two approaches is suggested:

Approach 1: Limit your coverage to fifteen vocabulary chapters, one a week.

In part of the one class hour you spend on vocabulary, go over the first four or six pages in class, using a method similar to the one we have described on pages 2–3 of this manual. Assign the last part of the chapter for homework. Then, as the first item of business in the next class, review those final pages. Follow up the review with the appropriate mastery test from the manual.

If only fifteen chapters are covered, and there is a second course in the reading sequence at your school, the book can be continued and completed in that second course.

Approach 2: Cover fifteen vocabulary chapters—three from each unit—in class, and assign the remaining chapters as homework. Then, at the end of each unit, give students one of the three *GBV* unit tests in the book or one of the following *VB* unit review activities in the book: "Choosing the Best Word to Complete an Item," "Adding a Word to an Item," or "Finding the Same or the Opposite Meaning." This procedure will enable you to hold students responsible for the outside-of-class vocabulary chapters as well.

You might want to tell students in advance that you will give them one of the three unit tests or unit review activities. However, don't tell them *which* of the three you will give. Encourage them, in other words, to review all of the words in the unit materials.

If there is not enough time in class to give the unit tests or unit review activities, you can ask students to do all of them at home. Then, in class, collect and grade *one* of the three. (Again, students should not know which of the three you will collect. That way, they will have to assume responsibility for learning all of the words.)

ABOUT THE COMPUTER DISKS

A computer disk in IBM (both MS-DOS and Windows) or Macintosh format will be available for each book. This disk will provide at least one additional multiple-choice test for each of the vocabulary chapters. The disk, with unlimited copying privileges, will be available at no charge to departments adopting at least 50 copies of the book.

Probably in no other area of reading instruction is the computer more useful than in reinforcing vocabulary. This vocabulary program takes advantage of the computer's unique capabilities and motivational appeal. Here are some features of the Townsend Press vocabulary disks:

- To aid pronunciation, the computer will pronounce each word aloud as many times as the students may request.

- After choosing an answer, students receive immediate feedback. The computer tells the student if the answer is right or wrong—and why.

- Every answer is followed by a brief explanation of that answer. Such explanations help ensure learning. The program, therefore, *teaches* as well as *tests*.

- Frequent use is made of the user's first name—a highly motivational word to any student!

- A sound option "rewards" each correct answer.

- A running score appears at the bottom of the screen, so the user always knows how well he or she is doing.

- A score file shows the user's final scores on each test. This score file may be accessed by instructors and printed out in any word processing program.

A FINAL NOTE

We invite you to write or otherwise communicate to us about your experiences in using the vocabulary books. This series is not a static project; we intend to revise it on a regular basis, responding to your suggestions and comments as well as our own continuing classroom experiences with the texts. To contact us, send us a note via our website (townsendpress.com), E-mail us at TPATNJ@aol.com or write to the Vocabulary Series Editor, Townsend Press, Pavilions at Greentree—408, Marlton, NJ 08053. By learning your reactions and those of your students, we can work at making what we feel are very good books even better.

Answers to the Chapter Activities in *VOCABULARY BASICS*

Chapter 1 (The Nose Knows; Barbie: A Bad Example?)

Learning Eight New Words		Matching Words with Meanings		Adding One Word to an Item		Adding Two Words to an Item	Showing You Understand the Words		Adding Words to a Reading	
1. c	5. a	1. 2	5. 7	1. a	5. e	1–2. h, e	1. c	5. b	1. a	5. d
2. b	6. a	2. 5	6. 6	2. b	6. f	3–4. a, d	2. a	6. a	2. c	6. c
3. c	7. a	3. 8	7. 3	3. c	7. d	5–6. c, b	3. b	7. b	3. b	7. a
4. b	8. c	4. 4	8. 1	4. g	8. h	7–8. g, f	4. b	8. b	4. d	8. b

Chapter 2 (Feeling Blue; A Late Love Letter)

Learning Eight New Words		Matching Words with Meanings		Adding One Word to an Item		Adding Two Words to an Item	Showing You Understand the Words		Adding Words to a Reading	
1. c	5. b	1. 5	5. 7	1. h	5. f	1–2. a, h	1. b	5. c	1. d	5. c
2. c	6. c	2. 3	6. 6	2. g	6. d	3–4. c, e	2. b	6. a	2. c	6. d
3. b	7. a	3. 4	7. 8	3. a	7. e	5–6. d, b	3. c	7. a	3. a	7. a
4. c	8. c	4. 1	8. 2	4. c	8. b	7–8. f, g	4. a	8. c	4. b	8. b

Chapter 3 (Ads That Lie; Horrible Hiccups!)

Learning Eight New Words		Matching Words with Meanings		Adding One Word to an Item		Adding Two Words to an Item	Showing You Understand the Words		Adding Words to a Reading	
1. b	5. b	1. 6	5. 4	1. e	5. g	1–2. g, d	1. a	5. c	1. c	5. c
2. a	6. c	2. 8	6. 1	2. c	6. h	3–4. f, a	2. b	6. a	2. a	6. a
3. a	7. b	3. 7	7. 3	3. b	7. d	5–6. c, e	3. a	7. c	3. b	7. b
4. c	8. c	4. 5	8. 2	4. a	8. f	7–8. b, h	4. c	8. a	4. d	8. d

Chapter 4 (An Upsetting Dream; A King's Mistake)

Learning Eight New Words		Matching Words with Meanings		Adding One Word to an Item		Adding Two Words to an Item	Showing You Understand the Words		Adding Words to a Reading	
1. b	5. c	1. 5	5. 6	1. a	5. d	1–2. a, f	1. b	5. a	1. c	5. b
2. a	6. a	2. 7	6. 4	2. f	6. g	3–4. c, g	2. a	6. b	2. d	6. d
3. c	7. c	3. 8	7. 3	3. c	7. h	5–6. e, b	3. b	7. b	3. a	7. c
4. c	8. a	4. 1	8. 2	4. e	8. b	7–8. d, h	4. c	8. c	4. b	8. a

Chapter 5 (Be Proud of Your Age!; Making Anger Work for You)

Learning Eight New Words		Matching Words with Meanings		Adding One Word to an Item		Adding Two Words to an Item	Showing You Understand the Words		Adding Words to a Reading	
1. a	5. c	1. 5	5. 1	1. d	5. c	1–2. a, f	1. a	5. c	1. c	5. a
2. c	6. c	2. 8	6. 7	2. a	6. h	3–4. e, g	2. c	6. a	2. b	6. c
3. a	7. a	3. 2	7. 4	3. e	7. g	5–6. h, c	3. a	7. b	3. d	7. b
4. b	8. c	4. 3	8. 6	4. b	8. f	7–8. d, b	4. c	8. a	4. a	8. d

Chapter 6 (How Not to Treat Customers; Stuck in the Middle)

Learning Eight New Words		Matching Words with Meanings		Adding One Word to an Item		Adding Two Words to an Item	Showing You Understand the Words		Adding Words to a Reading	
1. a	5. b	1. 6	5. 3	1. b	5. e	1–2. f, d	1. c	5. b	1. b	5. d
2. c	6. c	2. 4	6. 8	2. d	6. a	3–4. b, a	2. b	6. b	2. c	6. b
3. b	7. a	3. 5	7. 7	3. h	7. f	5–6. h, g	3. a	7. b	3. d	7. a
4. a	8. c	4. 2	8. 1	4. c	8. g	7–8. e, c	4. b	8. c	4. a	8. c

Chapter 7 (The Joy of Ice Cream; A Noisy Apartment)

Learning Eight New Words		Matching Words with Meanings		Adding One Word to an Item		Adding Two Words to an Item	Showing You Understand the Words		Adding Words to a Reading	
1. c	5. b	1. 4	5. 3	1. c	5. d	1–2. h, g	1. c	5. a	1. a	5. c
2. a	6. a	2. 7	6. 6	2. e	6. a	3–4. b, c	2. a	6. c	2. d	6. a
3. b	7. b	3. 1	7. 8	3. f	7. b	5–6. f, d	3. c	7. c	3. c	7. b
4. c	8. c	4. 2	8. 5	4. g	8. h	7–8. a, e	4. b	8. b	4. b	8. d

Chapter 8 (Nuts in the Senate; Calling Dr. Leech)

Learning Eight New Words		Matching Words with Meanings		Adding One Word to an Item		Adding Two Words to an Item	Showing You Understand the Words		Adding Words to a Reading	
1. b	5. a	1. 6	5. 7	1. f	5. d	1–2. h, b	1. b	5. b	1. b	5. b
2. b	6. b	2. 3	6. 2	2. a	6. g	3–4. a, c	2. b	6. c	2. d	6. d
3. c	7. c	3. 1	7. 5	3. e	7. h	5–6. g, f	3. b	7. a	3. a	7. a
4. c	8. c	4. 8	8. 4	4. c	8. b	7–8. e, d	4. c	8. c	4. c	8. c

Chapter 9 (TV and Violence; Are You Ready for a Pet?)

#	Learning Eight New Words	Matching Words with Meanings	Adding One Word to an Item	Adding Two Words to an Item	Showing You Understand the Words	Adding Words to a Reading
1	b	2	e	1–2. a, b	c	d
2	a	5	c		a	c
3	b	1	a	3–4. f, d	c	a
4	c	7	g		b	b
5	c	8	b	5–6. e, c	b	b
6	a	3	f		c	c
7	b	6	d	7–8. g, h	b	d
8	c	4	h		a	a

Chapter 10 (Help for Shy People; Not a Laughing Matter)

#	Learning Eight New Words	Matching Words with Meanings	Adding One Word to an Item	Adding Two Words to an Item	Showing You Understand the Words	Adding Words to a Reading
1	c	4	f	1–2. d, c	a	d
2	b	5	b		b	a
3	b	6	d	3–4. g, b	a	c
4	a	2	a		b	b
5	c	7	e	5–6. e, h	a	b
6	b	1	c		b	a
7	c	3	g	7–8. a, f	c	d
8	a	8	h		b	c

Chapter 11 (Taking Risks; Bad Manners Hurt Everyone)

#	Learning Eight New Words	Matching Words with Meanings	Adding One Word to an Item	Adding Two Words to an Item	Showing You Understand the Words	Adding Words to a Reading
1	a	5	c	1–2. g, h	a	a
2	b	2	g		a	c
3	c	3	b	3–4. e, c	c	b
4	c	6	a		b	d
5	c	4	h	5–6. a, f	c	a
6	b	8	d		a	b
7	c	1	f	7–8. d, b	b	c
8	a	7	e		b	d

Chapter 12 (Two Different Sisters; How "Honest Abe" Earned His Name)

#	Learning Eight New Words	Matching Words with Meanings	Adding One Word to an Item	Adding Two Words to an Item	Showing You Understand the Words	Adding Words to a Reading
1	b	6	b	1–2. d, e	c	d
2	a	8	e		a	b
3	c	1	a	3–4. a, c	c	c
4	c	4	c		b	a
5	b	5	f	5–6. g, b	a	d
6	b	3	d		b	a
7	c	2	g	7–8. f, h	a	b
8	a	7	h		a	c

Chapter 13 (Ready to Do Well; Advertising for a Date)

#	Learning Eight New Words	Matching Words with Meanings	Adding One Word to an Item	Adding Two Words to an Item	Showing You Understand the Words	Adding Words to a Reading
1	a	7	b	1–2. b, e	c	d
2	c	3	e		b	a
3	c	8	f	3–4. a, d	b	c
4	a	1	h		c	b
5	b	6	d	5–6. f, c	c	c
6	a	4	c		a	b
7	a	5	a	7–8. g, h	b	d
8	c	2	g		b	a

Chapter 14 (The Good and Bad Sides of Malls; As Good As It Looks?)

#	Learning Eight New Words	Matching Words with Meanings	Adding One Word to an Item	Adding Two Words to an Item	Showing You Understand the Words	Adding Words to a Reading
1	b	3	c	1–2. a, f	b	c
2	c	5	f		a	b
3	a	2	a	3–4. g, b	b	d
4	c	6	e		c	a
5	b	7	h	5–6. h, c	c	b
6	a	1	b		b	d
7	a	8	d	7–8. e, d	a	a
8	c	4	g		c	c

Chapter 15 (A Belief in Flying; She Tries Before She Buys)

#	Learning Eight New Words	Matching Words with Meanings	Adding One Word to an Item	Adding Two Words to an Item	Showing You Understand the Words	Adding Words to a Reading
1	a	2	d	1–2. a, c	c	a
2	c	1	b		b	c
3	a	4	a	3–4. d, f	b	b
4	b	3	f		b	d
5	b	7	h	5–6. e, g	c	a
6	c	8	e		a	b
7	b	6	c	7–8. b, h	a	c
8	a	5	g		b	d

Chapter 16 (Play Now, Pay Later; A Man of Many Faces)

#	Learning Eight New Words	Matching Words with Meanings	Adding One Word to an Item	Adding Two Words to an Item	Showing You Understand the Words	Adding Words to a Reading
1	c	6	g	1–2. a, c	b	c
2	c	5	f		c	b
3	b	4	d	3–4. f, e	a	d
4	c	3	e		c	a
5	a	7	c	5–6. g, d	c	a
6	b	1	a		c	c
7	a	2	b	7–8. h, b	b	b
8	c	8	h		a	d

Chapter 17 (Soaps Are for Me!; Keeping the Customer Happy)

Learning Eight New Words	Matching Words with Meanings	Adding One Word to an Item	Adding Two Words to an Item	Showing You Understand the Words	Adding Words to a Reading
1. c 5. c	1. 1 5. 5	1. c 5. e	1–2. g, e	1. c 5. b	1. b 5. b
2. b 6. b	2. 4 6. 6	2. h 6. a	3–4. d, f	2. b 6. a	2. a 6. a
3. a 7. b	3. 3 7. 2	3. b 7. d	5–6. a, c	3. c 7. a	3. d 7. d
4. a 8. c	4. 8 8. 7	4. f 8. g	7–8. b, h	4. a 8. c	4. c 8. c

Chapter 18 (A Fake "Cure"; The Jobs Everyone Hates)

Learning Eight New Words	Matching Words with Meanings	Adding One Word to an Item	Adding Two Words to an Item	Showing You Understand the Words	Adding Words to a Reading
1. a 5. c	1. 6 5. 2	1. f 5. d	1–2. e, b	1. c 5. a	1. d 5. b
2. c 6. a	2. 4 6. 5	2. a 6. e	3–4. h, g	2. a 6. c	2. c 6. d
3. b 7. c	3. 1 7. 8	3. h 7. g	5–6. a, d	3. b 7. a	3. a 7. a
4. c 8. b	4. 7 8. 3	4. c 8. b	7–8. c, f	4. b 8. b	4. b 8. c

Chapter 19 (A Young Librarian; No More Harm)

Learning Eight New Words	Matching Words with Meanings	Adding One Word to an Item	Adding Two Words to an Item	Showing You Understand the Words	Adding Words to a Reading
1. a 5. b	1. 4 5. 7	1. b 5. c	1–2. e, d	1. c 5. b	1. b 5. c
2. c 6. c	2. 5 6. 2	2. f 6. h	3–4. a, h	2. b 6. c	2. a 6. a
3. b 7. c	3. 3 7. 6	3. g 7. d	5–6. c, b	3. b 7. b	3. d 7. d
4. a 8. a	4. 8 8. 1	4. a 8. e	7–8. f, g	4. a 8. b	4. c 8. b

Chapter 20 (Is He Man or Machine?; Struck by Lightning)

Learning Eight New Words	Matching Words with Meanings	Adding One Word to an Item	Adding Two Words to an Item	Showing You Understand the Words	Adding Words to a Reading
1. b 5. a	1. 4 5. 2	1. a 5. g	1–2. a, b	1. c 5. b	1. b 5. b
2. a 6. b	2. 5 6. 6	2. c 6. h	3–4. d, f	2. a 6. b	2. c 6. d
3. b 7. a	3. 3 7. 7	3. d 7. b	5–6. c, h	3. c 7. c	3. d 7. c
4. c 8. a	4. 1 8. 8	4. f 8. e	7–8. e, g	4. b 8. b	4. a 8. a

Chapter 21 (Whose Fault Is It?; Forests Full of Life)

Learning Eight New Words	Matching Words with Meanings	Adding One Word to an Item	Adding Two Words to an Item	Showing You Understand the Words	Adding Words to a Reading
1. a 5. c	1. 8 5. 1	1. e 5. b	1–2. b, g	1. c 5. c	1. c 5. a
2. a 6. c	2. 4 6. 6	2. h 6. c	3–4. h, d	2. a 6. a	2. b 6. c
3. b 7. b	3. 2 7. 3	3. d 7. f	5–6. a, f	3. b 7. c	3. d 7. b
4. a 8. c	4. 7 8. 5	4. g 8. a	7–8. e, c	4. c 8. b	4. a 8. d

Chapter 22 (An Animal in Danger; The Simple Life of the Amish)

Learning Eight New Words	Matching Words with Meanings	Adding One Word to an Item	Adding Two Words to an Item	Showing You Understand the Words	Adding Words to a Reading
1. a 5. b	1. 4 5. 1	1. a 5. f	1–2. e, a	1. a 5. b	1. b 5. d
2. c 6. c	2. 6 6. 2	2. c 6. e	3–4. c, h	2. b 6. a	2. c 6. c
3. a 7. c	3. 7 7. 3	3. d 7. g	5–6. d, f	3. c 7. c	3. a 7. b
4. b 8. a	4. 5 8. 8	4. h 8. b	7–8. b, g	4. b 8. a	4. d 8. a

Chapter 23 (Taking a Break with TV; Working and Living Together)

Learning Eight New Words	Matching Words with Meanings	Adding One Word to an Item	Adding Two Words to an Item	Showing You Understand the Words	Adding Words to a Reading
1. b 5. c	1. 2 5. 7	1. e 5. h	1–2. b, e	1. a 5. a	1. d 5. c
2. c 6. a	2. 3 6. 8	2. a 6. c	3–4. d, c	2. a 6. a	2. b 6. d
3. c 7. c	3. 5 7. 6	3. f 7. g	5–6. h, f	3. b 7. c	3. c 7. a
4. a 8. c	4. 4 8. 1	4. b 8. d	7–8. g, a	4. b 8. b	4. a 8. b

Chapter 24 (The Horror of Hate; Taking Time for Thanks)

Learning Eight New Words	Matching Words with Meanings	Adding One Word to an Item	Adding Two Words to an Item	Showing You Understand the Words	Adding Words to a Reading
1. c 5. a	1. 1 5. 5	1. d 5. b	1–2. c, b	1. c 5. b	1. b 5. c
2. c 6. c	2. 6 6. 8	2. g 6. f	3–4. e, d	2. c 6. b	2. d 6. b
3. a 7. a	3. 2 7. 4	3. e 7. a	5–6. a, h	3. a 7. a	3. c 7. d
4. b 8. a	4. 7 8. 3	4. h 8. c	7–8. f, g	4. c 8. c	4. a 8. a

Chapter 25 (A Surprising Change; Just for Fun)

Learning Eight New Words		Matching Words with Meanings		Adding One Word to an Item		Adding Two Words to an Item	Showing You Understand the Words		Adding Words to a Reading	
1. b	5. c	1. 6	5. 8	1. g	5. d	1–2. g, c	1. c	5. c	1. d	5. c
2. c	6. c	2. 5	6. 4	2. b	6. e	3–4. a, h	2. a	6. a	2. c	6. a
3. a	7. a	3. 7	7. 1	3. h	7. c	5–6. d, b	3. c	7. c	3. b	7. d
4. a	8. c	4. 2	8. 3	4. a	8. f	7–8. e, f	4. b	8. a	4. a	8. b

Chapter 26 (Little Lies; Rudeness at the Movies)

Learning Eight New Words		Matching Words with Meanings		Adding One Word to an Item		Adding Two Words to an Item	Showing You Understand the Words		Adding Words to a Reading	
1. a	5. b	1. 7	5. 2	1. e	5. d	1–2. h, d	1. c	5. a	1. b	5. a
2. c	6. c	2. 3	6. 1	2. a	6. c	3–4. c, f	2. b	6. c	2. a	6. c
3. c	7. a	3. 6	7. 4	3. b	7. f	5–6. e, b	3. a	7. b	3. c	7. b
4. c	8. b	4. 8	8. 5	4. g	8. h	7–8. g, a	4. a	8. a	4. d	8. d

Chapter 27 (The Truth About Drinking; A Life Out of Balance)

Learning Eight New Words		Matching Words with Meanings		Adding One Word to an Item		Adding Two Words to an Item	Showing You Understand the Words		Adding Words to a Reading	
1. c	5. b	1. 2	5. 8	1. b	5. a	1–2. g, e	1. c	5. b	1. a	5. b
2. a	6. c	2. 5	6. 6	2. e	6. h	3–4. d, h	2. b	6. a	2. b	6. a
3. a	7. b	3. 7	7. 1	3. c	7. f	5–6. c, f	3. a	7. c	3. c	7. c
4. c	8. c	4. 3	8. 4	4. g	8. d	7–8. a, b	4. c	8. b	4. d	8. d

Chapter 28 (Animals Were First; Call Waiting—Oh, No!)

Learning Eight New Words		Matching Words with Meanings		Adding One Word to an Item		Adding Two Words to an Item	Showing You Understand the Words		Adding Words to a Reading	
1. b	5. c	1. 4	5. 3	1. c	5. e	1–2. d, c	1. b	5. c	1. a	5. a
2. b	6. c	2. 8	6. 5	2. b	6. f	3–4. b, a	2. c	6. b	2. c	6. d
3. c	7. c	3. 1	7. 7	3. g	7. a	5–6. h, f	3. c	7. a	3. b	7. c
4. a	8. b	4. 6	8. 2	4. d	8. h	7–8. e, g	4. c	8. a	4. d	8. b

Chapter 29 (A Cab Driver for Now; Thoughts at the Mall)

Learning Eight New Words		Matching Words with Meanings		Adding One Word to an Item		Adding Two Words to an Item	Showing You Understand the Words		Adding Words to a Reading	
1. b	5. c	1. 1	5. 8	1. g	5. f	1–2. d, f	1. c	5. c	1. d	5. a
2. c	6. c	2. 6	6. 3	2. e	6. h	3–4. e, b	2. b	6. b	2. b	6. c
3. a	7. a	3. 4	7. 7	3. b	7. a	5–6. h, c	3. c	7. b	3. a	7. d
4. b	8. c	4. 5	8. 2	4. c	8. d	7–8. a, g	4. a	8. a	4. c	8. b

Chapter 30 (The Birth of the American Red Cross; To Spank or Not to Spank?)

Learning Eight New Words		Matching Words with Meanings		Adding One Word to an Item		Adding Two Words to an Item	Showing You Understand the Words		Adding Words to a Reading	
1. c	5. a	1. 4	5. 5	1. h	5. f	1–2. d, e	1. b	5. c	1. a	5. c
2. b	6. c	2. 6	6. 1	2. a	6. d	3–4. a, c	2. c	6. b	2. d	6. b
3. c	7. b	3. 8	7. 3	3. e	7. g	5–6. b, f	3. c	7. a	3. c	7. a
4. c	8. c	4. 2	8. 7	4. c	8. b	7–8. h, g	4. b	8. a	4. b	8. d

VOCABULARY BASICS

Pretest

NAME: _____

SECTION: _____ DATE: _____

SCORE: _____

This test contains 100 items. In the space provided, write the letter of the choice that is closest in meaning to the **boldfaced** word.

Important: Keep in mind that this test is for diagnostic purposes only. **If you do not know a word, leave the space blank rather than guess at it.**

_____ 1. An **agreement** is:　　**a**) a fight　　**b**) a question　　**c**) an understanding

_____ 2. A **curious** person is:　　**a**) not interested　　**b**) angry　　**c**) full of questions

_____ 3. To **prepare** means:　　**a**) to get ready　　**b**) to watch　　**c**) to leave

_____ 4. If you **suggest** something, you:　　**a**) are afraid of it　　**b**) forget it　　**c**) offer an idea

_____ 5. To **entertain** means:　　**a**) to change　　**b**) to make sleepy　　**c**) to make happy

_____ 6. Something **negative** is:　　**a**) nice　　**b**) bad　　**c**) interesting

_____ 7. **Tension** is:　　**a**) rest　　**b**) happiness　　**c**) a nervous feeling

_____ 8. The **conclusion** of something is:　　**a**) the last part　　**b**) the best part　　**c**) the first part

_____ 9. A **volunteer** is:　　**a**) a bad worker　　**b**) a paid worker　　**c**) a worker who is not paid

_____ 10. Someone who is **fortunate** is:　　**a**) sorry　　**b**) scared　　**c**) lucky

_____ 11. If you **produce** something, you:　　**a**) make it　　**b**) break it　　**c**) take it

_____ 12. An **event** is:　　**a**) a problem　　**b**) something that happens　　**c**) a special skill

_____ 13. If something is **precious**, it:　　**a**) has great value　　**b**) is not important　　**c**) is funny

_____ 14. **Claim** means:　　**a**) to say something is true　　**b**) to hide　　**c**) to forget to say

_____ 15. To **satisfy** is to:　　**a**) surprise　　**b**) make unhappy　　**c**) be enough for

_____ 16. Something **definite** is:　　**a**) certain　　**b**) not fair　　**c**) wrong

_____ 17. **Specific** means:　　**a**) boring　　**b**) exact　　**c**) future

_____ 18. If you are **motivated**, you are:　　**a**) interested and excited　　**b**) well-known　　**c**) good-looking

_____ 19. To **suspect** is to:　　**a**) hope　　**b**) put away　　**c**) think

_____ 20. An **occasion** is:　　**a**) a car　　**b**) a special time　　**c**) a boring time

_____ 21. **Ability** means:　　**a**) a feeling of thanks　　**b**) a special skill　　**c**) a wish

_____ 22. If you **devour** something, you:　　**a**) make it　　**b**) eat it quickly　　**c**) save it for later

_____ 23. Something that is **constant** is:　　**a**) never-ending　　**b**) quiet　　**c**) sad

_____ 24. **Gratitude** means:　　**a**) anger　　**b**) thanks　　**c**) worry

_____ 25. A **struggle** is:　　**a**) a boring time　　**b**) an easy time　　**c**) a difficult time

(Continues on next page)

_____ 26. A good **excuse** is a good: **a)** reason   **b)** time   **c)** question

_____ 27. A **sociable** person is: **a)** quiet   **b)** friendly   **c)** angry

_____ 28. If something is **modern**, it is: **a)** up-to-date   **b)** broken down   **c)** strong

_____ 29. If you **ignore** something, you: **a)** know it   **b)** pay no attention to it   **c)** need it

_____ 30. **Inspire** means:
a) to stop someone from doing something
b) to make someone afraid to do something
c) to make someone want to do something

_____ 31. **Damage** means: **a)** hard work   **b)** safety   **c)** harm

_____ 32. Someone who is **capable**:   **a)** has skill   **b)** is not ready   **c)** is not careful

_____ 33. If you **require** something, you: **a)** send it away   **b)** do without it   **c)** need it

_____ 34. An **opportunity** is: **a)** a problem   **b)** a habit   **c)** a chance

_____ 35. If you are **sensitive**, you are: **a)** not caring   **b)** happy   **c)** understanding

_____ 36. To **persist** means: **a)** to give up easily   **b)** to keep doing something
c) to forget

_____ 37. Something **insulting** is: **a)** kind   **b)** easy to understand   **c)** hurtful

_____ 38. If you are **comfortable**, you are: **a)** relaxed   **b)** mean   **c)** thirsty

_____ 39. **Allow** means: **a)** to hate   **b)** to let   **c)** to stop

_____ 40. If you **avoid** something, you: **a)** get closer to it   **b)** keep away from it   **c)** enjoy it

_____ 41. **Confident** people are: **a)** mean   **b)** honest   **c)** sure of themselves

_____ 42. To **donate** something is to: **a)** show it off   **b)** find it   **c)** give it away

_____ 43. If something **disgusts** you, it: **a)** makes you happy   **b)** makes you sick   **c)** keeps you busy

_____ 44. **Advice** is: **a)** a helpful idea   **b)** a friendship   **c)** a mistake

_____ 45. If something is **impossible**, it: **a)** happens all the time   **b)** cannot happen   **c)** is safe

_____ 46. **Necessary** means: **a)** not wanted   **b)** careful   **c)** very important

_____ 47. **Defeat** means: **a)** to beat in a contest   **b)** to keep   **c)** to hide

_____ 48. If you **regret** something, you: **a)** feel bad about it   **b)** are thankful for it
c) are nervous about it

_____ 49. An **opinion** is: **a)** a thought   **b)** a need   **c)** a job

_____ 50. **Encourage** means: **a)** to stop   **b)** to shout at angrily   **c)** to give hope to

(Continues on next page)

_____ 51. If you **prevent** something, you: **a)** stop it ahead of time   **b)** help it   **c)** give it away

_____ 52. Something that is **available** is: **a)** boring   **b)** easy to get   **c)** expensive

_____ 53. A **portion** is: **a)** all of something   **b)** nothing   **c)** a part of something

_____ 54. When you **arrange** things, you: **a)** buy them   **b)** mix them up   **c)** put them in order

_____ 55. If you **depend** on people, you: **a)** wait for them   **b)** rely on them   **c)** turn away from them

_____ 56. A **cautious** person is: **a)** happy   **b)** tired   **c)** careful

_____ 57. **Contain** means: **a)** to dislike   **b)** to make   **c)** to have inside

_____ 58. If you are **uncertain**, you are: **a)** not interested   **b)** sure   **c)** not sure

_____ 59. **Effort** means: **a)** hard work   **b)** sadness   **c)** good looks

_____ 60. Something that is **effective** is: **a)** late   **b)** slow   **c)** good

_____ 61. To **collapse** means: **a)** to build   **b)** to stay safe   **c)** to fall down

_____ 62. When you are **relieved**, you are: **a)** unhappy   **b)** not caring   **c)** less worried

_____ 63. Things that are **similar** are: **a)** not safe   **b)** good-looking   **c)** like each other

_____ 64. **Confusion** is: **a)** a feeling of danger   **b)** a feeling of not knowing what to do   **c)** a feeling of peace

_____ 65. Something that is **distant** is: **a)** nearby   **b)** far away   **c)** different

_____ 66. To **refuse** means: **a)** to decide not to   **b)** to forget about   **c)** to want to

_____ 67. **Humor** is: **a)** a lesson   **b)** anger   **c)** something funny

_____ 68. Someone who is **stubborn**:   **a)** is easy to get along with   **b)** does not want to do something   **c)** is quick to learn

_____ 69. To **increase** means: **a)** to make smaller   **b)** to make greater   **c)** to get rid of

_____ 70. **Progress** is: **a)** mistakes   **b)** friends   **c)** movement toward a goal

_____ 71. A **generous** person is: **a)** willing to share   **b)** selfish   **c)** bad-tempered

_____ 72. If you **select** something, you: **a)** break it   **b)** lose it   **c)** choose it

_____ 73. Something that is **scarce** is: **a)** easily found   **b)** famous   **c)** few in number

_____ 74. **Imagine** means: **a)** to picture in the mind   **b)** to forget   **c)** to say something nice

_____ 75. Something **familiar** is: **a)** far away   **b)** well-known   **c)** sad

(Continues on next page)

_____ 76. A **detail** is: **a)** the end of something   **b)** a small part   **c)** a color

_____ 77. **Persuade** means: **a)** to get someone to do something   **b)** to stop   **c)** to leave

_____ 78. To **occupy** something means: **a)** to break it   **b)** to clean it   **c)** to live in it

_____ 79. To **realize** is to: **a)** hope   **b)** know   **c)** write

_____ 80. If you **separate** things, you: **a)** bring them together   **b)** make them larger
     c) put them in different places

_____ 81. Something that is **common**:   **a)** is very large   **b)** is strange   **c)** happens often

_____ 82. **Condition** means: **a)** the shape something is in   **b)** a neighborhood   **c)** news

_____ 83. To **develop** means: **a)** to grow a little at a time   **b)** to leave   **c)** to dry

_____ 84. Your **duty** is your: **a)** job   **b)** hobby   **c)** problem

_____ 85. To **pretend** is to: **a)** make believe   **b)** grow   **c)** know

_____ 86. Something that is **permanent** is: **a)** good   **b)** new   **c)** long-lasting

_____ 87. An **injury** is: **a)** a movement   **b)** something that hurts   **c)** good health

_____ 88. If you **expect** something, you: **a)** dislike it   **b)** want it   **c)** believe it will happen

_____ 89. Someone who is **competent** is: **a)** dangerous   **b)** good at something   **c)** boring

_____ 90. A **request** is a: **a)** problem   **b)** answer   **c)** thing that is asked for

_____ 91. If you **succeed**, you: **a)** do badly   **b)** do well   **c)** pay too much

_____ 92. To **examine** means: **a)** to leave   **b)** to use   **c)** to look at carefully

_____ 93. To **recognize** is to: **a)** know from before   **b)** study   **c)** lose

_____ 94. The **value** of something is: **a)** the reason for it   **b)** its color   **c)** what it is worth

_____ 95. If something **seldom** happens, it: **a)** happens every day   **b)** does not happen often
     c) happens on purpose

_____ 96. If you **consider** something, you: **a)** cover it up   **b)** think about it   **c)** want it

_____ 97. To **admire** means: **a)** to laugh at   **b)** to think highly of   **c)** to forget

_____ 98. If you **attempt** something, you: **a)** repeat it   **b)** try it   **c)** remember it

_____ 99. A **solution** is: **a)** a reason for doing something   **b)** a question
     c) an answer to a problem

_____ 100. If you **achieve** something, you: **a)** lose it   **b)** have trouble with it   **c)** reach a goal

---

STOP. This is the end of the test. If there is time remaining, you may go back and recheck your answers. When the time is up, hand in both your answer sheet and this test booklet to your instructor.

Posttest

This test contains 100 items. In the space provided, write the letter of the choice that is closest in meaning to the **boldfaced** word.

_____ 1. If you **produce** something, you: **a)** take it   **b)** break it   **c)** make it

_____ 2. An **event** is: **a)** a special skill   **b)** a problem   **c)** something that happens

_____ 3. If something is **precious**, it: **a)** is not important   **b)** has great value   **c)** is funny

_____ 4. **Claim** means: **a)** to hide   **b)** to forget to say   **c)** to say something is true

_____ 5. To **satisfy** is to: **a)** make unhappy   **b)** be enough for   **c)** surprise

_____ 6. A **cautious** person is: **a)** careful   **b)** tired   **c)** happy

_____ 7. **Contain** means: **a)** to make   **b)** to have inside   **c)** to dislike

_____ 8. If you are **uncertain**, you are: **a)** not sure   **b)** not interested   **c)** sure

_____ 9. **Effort** means: **a)** good looks   **b)** sadness   **c)** hard work

_____ 10. Something that is **effective** is: **a)** slow   **b)** good   **c)** late

_____ 11. Something that is **common**:   **a)** happens often   **b)** is strange   **c)** is very large

_____ 12. **Condition** means: **a)** news   **b)** a neighborhood   **c)** the shape something is in

_____ 13. To **develop** means: **a)** to leave   **b)** to grow a little at a time   **c)** to dry

_____ 14. Your **duty** is your: **a)** hobby   **b)** job   **c)** problem

_____ 15. To **pretend** is to: **a)** know   **b)** grow   **c)** make believe

_____ 16. A good **excuse** is a good: **a)** time   **b)** reason   **c)** question

_____ 17. A **sociable** person is: **a)** quiet   **b)** angry   **c)** friendly

_____ 18. If something is **modern**, it is: **a)** strong   **b)** broken down   **c)** up-to-date

_____ 19. If you **ignore** something, you: **a)** need it   **b)** pay no attention to it   **c)** know it

_____ 20. If you **avoid** something, you: **a)** get closer to it   **b)** enjoy it   **c)** keep away from it

_____ 21. **Damage** means: **a)** harm   **b)** safety   **c)** hard work

_____ 22. Someone who is **capable**:   **a)** is not ready   **b)** is not careful   **c)** has skill

_____ 23. If you **require** something, you: **a)** need it   **b)** do without it   **c)** send it away

_____ 24. An **opportunity** is: **a)** a habit   **b)** a chance   **c)** a problem

_____ 25. If you are **sensitive**, you are: **a)** understanding   **b)** happy   **c)** not caring

(Continues on next page)

_____ 26. To **refuse** means: **a**) to want to   **b**) to forget about   **c**) to decide not to

_____ 27. **Humor** is: **a**) a lesson   **b**) something funny   **c**) anger

_____ 28. Someone who is **stubborn**:   **a**) does not want to do something   **b**) is easy to get along with   **c**) is quick to learn

_____ 29. To **increase** means: **a**) to make smaller   **b**) to get rid of   **c**) to make greater

_____ 30. **Progress** is: **a**) friends   **b**) movement toward a goal   **c**) mistakes

_____ 31. If you **succeed**, you: **a**) pay too much   **b**) do badly   **c**) do well

_____ 32. To **examine** means: **a**) to look at carefully   **b**) to use   **c**) to leave

_____ 33. To **recognize** is to: **a**) lose   **b**) study   **c**) know from before

_____ 34. The **value** of something is: **a**) what it is worth   **b**) its color   **c**) the reason for it

_____ 35. If something **seldom** happens, it: **a**) happens every day   **b**) happens on purpose   **c**) does not happen often

_____ 36. To **persist** means: **a**) to keep doing something   **b**) to give up easily   **c**) to forget

_____ 37. Something **insulting** is: **a**) kind   **b**) hurtful   **c**) easy to understand

_____ 38. If you are **comfortable**, you are: **a**) thirsty   **b**) mean   **c**) relaxed

_____ 39. **Allow** means: **a**) to stop   **b**) to let   **c**) to hate

_____ 40. **Inspire** means: **a**) to stop someone from doing something   **b**) to make someone want to do something   **c**) to make someone afraid to do something

_____ 41. If you **prevent** something, you: **a**) give it away   **b**) stop it ahead of time   **c**) help it

_____ 42. Something that is **available** is: **a**) boring   **b**) easy to get   **c**) expensive

_____ 43. A **portion** is: **a**) a part of something   **b**) nothing   **c**) all of something

_____ 44. When you **arrange** things, you: **a**) mix them up   **b**) put them in order   **c**) buy them

_____ 45. If you **depend** on people, you: **a**) turn away from them   **b**) wait for them   **c**) rely on them

_____ 46. **Necessary** means: **a**) very important   **b**) careful   **c**) not wanted

_____ 47. **Defeat** means: **a**) to keep   **b**) to beat in a contest   **c**) to hide

_____ 48. If you **regret** something, you: **a**) are thankful for it   **b**) feel bad about it   **c**) are nervous about it

_____ 49. An **opinion** is: **a**) a job   **b**) a need   **c**) a thought

_____ 50. **Encourage** means: **a**) to give hope to   **b**) to shout at angrily   **c**) to stop

(Continues on next page)

_____ 51. **Ability** means: **a)** a special skill   **b)** a feeling of thanks   **c)** a wish

_____ 52. If you **devour** something, you: **a)** make it   **b)** save it for later   **c)** eat it quickly

_____ 53. Something that is **constant** is: **a)** never-ending   **b)** sad   **c)** quiet

_____ 54. **Gratitude** means: **a)** anger   **b)** worry   **c)** thanks

_____ 55. A **struggle** is: **a)** a difficult time   **b)** an easy time   **c)** a boring time

_____ 56. A **detail** is: **a)** a color   **b)** a small part   **c)** the end of something

_____ 57. **Persuade** means: **a)** to stop   **b)** to get someone to do something   **c)** to leave

_____ 58. To **occupy** something means: **a)** to break it   **b)** to live in it   **c)** to clean it

_____ 59. To **realize** is to: **a)** know   **b)** hope   **c)** write

_____ 60. If you **separate** things, you: **a)** put them in different places   **b)** make them larger   **c)** bring them together

_____ 61. To **collapse** means: **a)** to build   **b)** to fall down   **c)** to stay safe

_____ 62. When you are **relieved**, you are: **a)** less worried   **b)** not caring   **c)** unhappy

_____ 63. Things that are **similar** are: **a)** not safe   **b)** like each other   **c)** good-looking

_____ 64. **Confusion** is: **a)** a feeling of not knowing what to do   **b)** a feeling of danger   **c)** a feeling of peace

_____ 65. Something that is **distant** is: **a)** nearby   **b)** different   **c)** far away

_____ 66. Something **negative** is: **a)** interesting   **b)** nice   **c)** bad

_____ 67. **Tension** is: **a)** rest   **b)** a nervous feeling   **c)** happiness

_____ 68. The **conclusion** of something is: **a)** the first part   **b)** the best part   **c)** the last part

_____ 69. A **volunteer** is: **a)** a paid worker   **b)** a worker who is not paid   **c)** a bad worker

_____ 70. Someone who is **fortunate** is: **a)** lucky   **b)** scared   **c)** sorry

_____ 71. **Confident** people are: **a)** sure of themselves   **b)** honest   **c)** mean

_____ 72. To **donate** something is to: **a)** find it   **b)** give it away   **c)** show it off

_____ 73. If something **disgusts** you, it: **a)** makes you happy   **b)** keeps you busy   **c)** makes you sick

_____ 74. **Advice** is: **a)** a friendship   **b)** a helpful idea   **c)** a mistake

_____ 75. If something is **impossible**, it: **a)** is safe   **b)** cannot happen   **c)** happens all the time

(Continues on next page)

_____ 76. If you **consider** something, you: **a)** think about it   **b)** cover it up   **c)** want it

_____ 77. To **admire** means: **a)** to laugh at   **b)** to forget   **c)** to think highly of

_____ 78. If you **attempt** something, you: **a)** try it   **b)** repeat it   **c)** remember it

_____ 79. A **solution** is: **a)** a question   **b)** an answer to a problem   **c)** a reason for doing something

_____ 80. If you **achieve** something, you: **a)** reach a goal   **b)** have trouble with it   **c)** lose it

_____ 81. An **agreement** is: **a)** a question   **b)** an understanding   **c)** a fight

_____ 82. A **curious** person is: **a)** full of questions   **b)** angry   **c)** not interested

_____ 83. To **prepare** means: **a)** to watch   **b)** to get ready   **c)** to leave

_____ 84. If you **suggest** something, you: **a)** offer an idea   **b)** forget it   **c)** are afraid of it

_____ 85. To **entertain** means: **a)** to change   **b)** to make happy   **c)** to make sleepy

_____ 86. Something that is **permanent** is: **a)** long-lasting   **b)** new   **c)** good

_____ 87. An **injury** is: **a)** something that hurts   **b)** a movement   **c)** good health

_____ 88. If you **expect** something, you: **a)** want it   **b)** believe it will happen   **c)** dislike it

_____ 89. Someone who is **competent** is: **a)** dangerous   **b)** boring   **c)** good at something

_____ 90. A **request** is a: **a)** problem   **b)** thing that is asked for   **c)** answer

_____ 91. A **generous** person is: **a)** bad-tempered   **b)** selfish   **c)** willing to share

_____ 92. If you **select** something, you: **a)** lose it   **b)** choose it   **c)** break it

_____ 93. Something that is **scarce** is: **a)** few in number   **b)** famous   **c)** easily found

_____ 94. **Imagine** means: **a)** to forget   **b)** to picture in the mind   **c)** to say something nice

_____ 95. Something **familiar** is: **a)** well-known   **b)** far away   **c)** sad

_____ 96. Something **definite** is: **a)** wrong   **b)** not fair   **c)** certain

_____ 97. **Specific** means: **a)** exact   **b)** boring   **c)** future

_____ 98. If you are **motivated**, you are: **a)** good-looking   **b)** well-known   **c)** interested and excited

_____ 99. To **suspect** is to: **a)** think   **b)** put away   **c)** hope

_____ 100. An **occasion** is: **a)** a car   **b)** a boring time   **c)** a special time

STOP. This is the end of the test. If there is time remaining, you may go back and recheck your answers. When the time is up, hand in both your answer sheet and this test booklet to your instructor.

Name: _____

In the space provided, write the letter of the choice that is closest in meaning to the **boldfaced** word.

_____ 1. **agreement**   **a)** a fight   **b)** a question   **c)** an understanding

_____ 2. **cancel**   **a)** to remember   **b)** to not do as planned   **c)** to get ready for

_____ 3. **curious**   **a)** not interested   **b)** angry   **c)** full of questions

_____ 4. **fact**   **a)** a rule   **b)** something true   **c)** a long story

_____ 5. **flexible**   **a)** able to bend   **b)** real   **c)** heavy

_____ 6. **odor**   **a)** a smell   **b)** a cost   **c)** a warm feeling

_____ 7. **prepare**   **a)** to get ready   **b)** to watch   **c)** to leave

_____ 8. **suggest**   **a)** to fear   **b)** to forget   **c)** to offer an idea

_____ 9. **daily**   **a)** happening each day   **b)** happening each week   **c)** happening each year

_____ 10. **entertain**   **a)** to change   **b)** to make sleepy   **c)** to make happy

_____ 11. **experience**   **a)** a difficult question   **b)** something that a person lives through
   c) a good reason

_____ 12. **identify**   **a)** to dislike   **b)** to make something out of something else
   c) to find out who someone is or what something is

_____ 13. **negative**   **a)** nice   **b)** bad   **c)** interesting

_____ 14. **original**   **a)** quiet   **b)** weak   **c)** new

_____ 15. **produce**   **a)** to make   **b)** to break   **c)** to take

_____ 16. **tension**   **a)** rest   **b)** happiness   **c)** a nervous feeling

_____ 17. **attack**   **a)** to run away   **b)** to hurt   **c)** to keep safe

_____ 18. **conclusion**   **a)** the last part   **b)** the best part   **c)** the first part

_____ 19. **event**   **a)** something that happens   **b)** a problem   **c)** a special skill

_____ 20. **humble**   **a)** loud   **b)** afraid   **c)** not bragging

_____ 21. **minor**   **a)** dangerous   **b)** small   **c)** important

_____ 22. **protect**   **a)** to hurt   **b)** to look at   **c)** to keep safe

_____ 23. **talent**   **a)** a dislike   **b)** a skill   **c)** a fear

_____ 24. **volunteer**   **a)** a bad worker   **b)** a paid worker   **c)** a worker who is not paid

(Continues on next page)

_____ 25. **accuse** **a)** to ask **b)** to blame **c)** to thank

_____ 26. **claim** **a)** to say that something is true **b)** to hide **c)** to forget to say

_____ 27. **embarrassed** **a)** proud **b)** easy to like **c)** ashamed

_____ 28. **inspire** **a)** to stop someone from doing something **b)** to make someone afraid to do something **c)** to make someone want to do something

_____ 29. **pleasant** **a)** sleepy **b)** mean **c)** nice

_____ 30. **precious** **a)** having great value **b)** not important **c)** funny

_____ 31. **public** **a)** secret **b)** not crowded **c)** open to everyone

_____ 32. **unusual** **a)** surprising **b)** helpful **c)** boring

_____ 33. **benefit** **a)** to help **b)** to harm **c)** to tell

_____ 34. **delay** **a)** to enjoy **b)** to hurry **c)** to wait until later

_____ 35. **emphasize** **a)** to show to be important **b)** to cover up **c)** to turn around

_____ 36. **logical** **a)** empty **b)** making sense **c)** lucky

_____ 37. **rival** **a)** someone that another person is working with
b) someone who is going to school
c) someone that another person tries to beat in a contest of some kind

_____ 38. **satisfy** **a)** to surprise **b)** to make unhappy **c)** to be enough for

_____ 39. **tempt** **a)** to invite someone to do something bad
b) to warn someone against doing something bad
c) to stop someone from doing something bad

_____ 40. **vacant** **a)** helpful **b)** crowded **c)** not in use

_____ 41. **definite** **a)** certain **b)** not fair **c)** wrong

_____ 42. **fortunate** **a)** sorry **b)** scared **c)** lucky

_____ 43. **leisure** **a)** hard work **b)** free time **c)** a deep sleep

_____ 44. **motivated** **a)** interested and excited **b)** well-known **c)** good-looking

_____ 45. **oppose** **a)** to be happy about **b)** to be against **c)** to speak about

_____ 46. **refer** **a)** to put a stop to **b)** to be unable to remember **c)** to talk about

_____ 47. **specific** **a)** exact **b)** boring **c)** future

_____ 48. **suspect** **a)** to hope **b)** to put away **c)** to think

---

SCORE: (Number correct _____ × 2) + 4 = _____ %

Unit 1: *Posttest*

In the space provided, write the letter of the choice that is closest in meaning to the **boldfaced** word.

_____ 1. **prepare**   a) to watch   b) to get ready   c) to leave

_____ 2. **suggest**   a) to fear   b) to forget   c) to offer an idea

_____ 3. **daily**   a) happening each year   b) happening each week   c) happening each day

_____ 4. **entertain**   a) to change   b) to make happy   c) to make sleepy

_____ 5. **experience**   a) something that a person lives through   b) a difficult question
          c) a good reason

_____ 6. **identify**   a) to make something out of something else   b) to find out who
          someone is or what something is   c) to dislike

_____ 7. **event**   a) a problem   b) something that happens   c) a special skill

_____ 8. **humble**   a) not bragging   b) loud   c) afraid

_____ 9. **minor**   a) dangerous   b) important   c) small

_____ 10. **protect**   a) to hurt   b) to keep safe   c) to look at

_____ 11. **talent**   a) a skill   b) a dislike   c) a fear

_____ 12. **volunteer**   a) a bad worker   b) a worker who is not paid   c) a paid worker

_____ 13. **negative**   a) bad   b) nice   c) interesting

_____ 14. **original**   a) quiet   b) new   c) weak

_____ 15. **produce**   a) to break   b) to make   c) to take

_____ 16. **tension**   a) rest   b) a nervous feeling   c) happiness

_____ 17. **attack**   a) to hurt   b) to run away   c) to keep safe

_____ 18. **conclusion**   a) the first part   b) the best part   c) the last part

_____ 19. **agreement**   a) a fight   b) an understanding   c) a question

_____ 20. **cancel**   a) to remember   b) to get ready for   c) to not do as planned

_____ 21. **curious**   a) not interested   b) full of questions   c) angry

_____ 22. **fact**   a) something true   b) a rule   c) a long story

_____ 23. **flexible**   a) real   b) able to bend   c) heavy

_____ 24. **odor**   a) a cost   b) a warm feeling   c) a smell

(Continues on next page)

_____ 25. **rival**   **a)** someone that another person is working with
b) someone that another person tries to beat in a contest of some kind
c) someone who is going to school

_____ 26. **satisfy**   **a)** to surprise   **b)** to be enough for   **c)** to make unhappy

_____ 27. **tempt**   **a)** to invite someone to do something bad
b) to warn someone against doing something bad
c) to stop someone from doing something bad

_____ 28. **vacant**   **a)** helpful   **b)** not in use   **c)** crowded

_____ 29. **definite**   **a)** not fair   **b)** wrong   **c)** certain

_____ 30. **fortunate**   **a)** sorry   **b)** lucky   **c)** scared

_____ 31. **public**   **a)** secret   **b)** open to everyone   **c)** not crowded

_____ 32. **unusual**   **a)** helpful   **b)** boring   **c)** surprising

_____ 33. **benefit**   **a)** to harm   **b)** to help   **c)** to tell

_____ 34. **delay**   **a)** to enjoy   **b)** to wait until later   **c)** to hurry

_____ 35. **emphasize**   **a)** to show to be important   **b)** to cover up   **c)** to turn around

_____ 36. **logical**   **a)** empty   **b)** lucky   **c)** making sense

_____ 37. **leisure**   **a)** a deep sleep   **b)** hard work   **c)** free time

_____ 38. **motivated**   **a)** well-known   **b)** interested and excited   **c)** good-looking

_____ 39. **oppose**   **a)** to be happy about   **b)** to speak about   **c)** to be against

_____ 40. **refer**   **a)** to talk about   **b)** to put a stop to   **c)** to be unable to remember

_____ 41. **specific**   **a)** boring   **b)** exact   **c)** future

_____ 42. **suspect**   **a)** to hope   **b)** to think   **c)** to put away

_____ 43. **accuse**   **a)** to ask   **b)** to thank   **c)** to blame

_____ 44. **claim**   **a)** to hide   **b)** to say that something is true   **c)** to forget to say

_____ 45. **embarrassed**   **a)** ashamed   **b)** proud   **c)** easy to like

_____ 46. **inspire**   **a)** to stop someone from doing something   **b)** to make someone want to do something   **c)** to make someone afraid to do something

_____ 47. **pleasant**   **a)** nice   **b)** mean   **c)** sleepy

_____ 48. **precious**   **a)** funny   **b)** not important   **c)** having great value

SCORE: (Number correct _____ × 2) + 4 = _____ %

Unit 2: *Pretest*

In the space provided, write the letter of the choice that is closest in meaning to the **boldfaced** word.

_____ 1. **aware**   a) sad about something   b) ashamed of something
c) knowing about something

_____ 2. **constant**   a) never-ending   b) quiet   c) sad

_____ 3. **devour**   a) to make   b) to eat quickly   c) to save for later

_____ 4. **discover**   a) to lose   b) to sell   c) to find

_____ 5. **distressed**   a) full of energy   b) upset   c) up-to-date

_____ 6. **modern**   a) up-to-date   b) broken down   c) strong

_____ 7. **occasion**   a) a car   b) a special time   c) a boring time

_____ 8. **popular**   a) healthy   b) not known   c) well-liked

_____ 9. **ability**   a) a feeling of thanks   b) a special skill   c) a wish

_____ 10. **create**   a) to study   b) to make   c) to look at quickly

_____ 11. **damage**   a) hard work   b) safety   c) harm

_____ 12. **failure**   a) something that works easily   b) something that works well
c) something that does not turn out well

_____ 13. **glance**   a) to look quickly   b) to listen carefully   c) to keep from looking

_____ 14. **gratitude**   a) anger   b) thanks   c) worry

_____ 15. **introduce**   a) sell something to someone   b) not agree with someone
c) meet someone for the first time

_____ 16. **labor**   a) space   b) quiet   c) hard work

_____ 17. **avoid**   a) to get closer to   b) to keep away from   c) to enjoy

_____ 18. **excuse**   a) a reason   b) a happy time   c) a question

_____ 19. **helpless**   a) not able to see well   b) not able to take care of oneself
c) not very well known

_____ 20. **include**   a) to be without   b) to stay away from   c) to be made up of

_____ 21. **intend**   a) to forget   b) to hate   c) to plan

_____ 22. **normal**   a) usual   b) strange   c) easily hurt

_____ 23. **sociable**   a) quiet   b) friendly   c) angry

_____ 24. **struggle**   a) a boring time   b) an easy time   c) a difficult time

_____ 25. **approach**   **a)** to go away from   **b)** to need   **c)** to come near

_____ 26. **damp**   **a)** clean   **b)** a little wet   **c)** good-smelling

_____ 27. **ignore**   **a)** to know   **b)** to pay no attention to   **c)** to need

_____ 28. **loyal**   **a)** faithful   **b)** mean   **c)** helpful

_____ 29. **numerous**   **a)** few   **b)** ugly   **c)** many

_____ 30. **previous**   **a)** next   **b)** earlier   **c)** favorite

_____ 31. **require**   **a)** to send away   **b)** to do without   **c)** to need

_____ 32. **timid**   **a)** shy   **b)** noisy   **c)** old

_____ 33. **capable**   **a)** having skill   **b)** not ready   **c)** not careful

_____ 34. **careless**   **a)** intelligent   **b)** not careful   **c)** cheerful

_____ 35. **furious**   **a)** helpful   **b)** quiet   **c)** angry

_____ 36. **observe**   **a)** to miss   **b)** to copy   **c)** to watch

_____ 37. **opportunity**   **a)** a problem   **b)** a habit   **c)** a chance

_____ 38. **resist**   **a)** to answer   **b)** to say no to   **c)** to invite

_____ 39. **reverse**   **a)** to say loudly   **b)** to keep   **c)** to turn around

_____ 40. **tradition**   **a)** a handed-down way of doing something   **b)** a fight   **c)** a difficult time

_____ 41. **allow**   **a)** to hate   **b)** to let   **c)** to stop

_____ 42. **comfortable**   **a)** relaxed   **b)** mean   **c)** thirsty

_____ 43. **distract**   **a)** to have questions about   **b)** to make clean   **c)** to take away attention

_____ 44. **insulting**   **a)** kind   **b)** easy to understand   **c)** hurtful

_____ 45. **persist**   **a)** to give up easily   **b)** to keep doing something   **c)** to forget

_____ 46. **respect**   **a)** a great happiness   **b)** a great liking   **c)** a great anger

_____ 47. **sensitive**   **a)** not caring   **b)** happy   **c)** understanding

_____ 48. **wonder**   **a)** to want to know   **b)** to answer   **c)** to blame

**SCORE:** (Number correct _____ × 2) + 4 = _____ %

Name: _____

Unit 2: *Posttest*

In the space provided, write the letter of the choice that is closest in meaning to the **boldfaced** word.

_____ 1. **intend**   **a)** to forget   **b)** to plan   **c)** to hate

_____ 2. **normal**   **a)** easily hurt   **b)** strange   **c)** usual

_____ 3. **sociable**   **a)** quiet   **b)** angry   **c)** friendly

_____ 4. **struggle**   **a)** a boring time   **b)** a difficult time   **c)** an easy time

_____ 5. **occasion**   **a)** a special time   **b)** a car   **c)** a boring time

_____ 6. **popular**   **a)** healthy   **b)** well-liked   **c)** not known

_____ 7. **ability**   **a)** a special skill   **b)** a feeling of thanks   **c)** a wish

_____ 8. **helpless**   **a)** not able to take care of oneself   **b)** not able to see well
                 c) not very well known

_____ 9. **include**   **a)** to be without   **b)** to be made up of   **c)** to stay away from

_____ 10. **aware**   **a)** knowing about something   **b)** ashamed of something
                 c) sad about something

_____ 11. **constant**   **a)** quiet   **b)** sad   **c)** never-ending

_____ 12. **create**   **a)** to look at quickly   **b)** to study   **c)** to make

_____ 13. **glance**   **a)** to listen carefully   **b)** to look quickly   **c)** to keep from looking

_____ 14. **gratitude**   **a)** anger   **b)** worry   **c)** thanks

_____ 15. **introduce**   **a)** meet someone for the first time   **b)** not agree with someone
                 c) sell something to someone

_____ 16. **damage**   **a)** safety   **b)** harm   **c)** hard work

_____ 17. **failure**   **a)** something that does not turn out well   **b)** something that works well
                 c) something that works easily

_____ 18. **labor**   **a)** hard work   **b)** quiet   **c)** space

_____ 19. **avoid**   **a)** to get closer to   **b)** to enjoy   **c)** to keep away from

_____ 20. **excuse**   **a)** a question   **b)** a happy time   **c)** a reason

_____ 21. **devour**   **a)** to eat quickly   **b)** to make   **c)** to save for later

_____ 22. **discover**   **a)** to lose   **b)** to find   **c)** to sell

_____ 23. **distressed**   **a)** full of energy   **b)** up-to-date   **c)** upset

_____ 24. **modern**   **a)** broken down   **b)** strong   **c)** up-to-date

(Continues on next page)

_____ 25. **persist**   a) to keep doing something   b) to give up easily   c) to forget

_____ 26. **reverse**   a) to turn around   b) to keep   c) to say loudly

_____ 27. **approach**   a) to go away from   b) to come near   c) to need

_____ 28. **damp**   a) clean   b) good-smelling   c) a little wet

_____ 29. **numerous**   a) many   b) ugly   c) few

_____ 30. **previous**   a) next   b) favorite   c) earlier

_____ 31. **require**   a) to send away   b) to need   c) to do without

_____ 32. **timid**   a) noisy   b) shy   c) old

_____ 33. **capable**   a) not careful   b) not ready   c) having skill

_____ 34. **careless**   a) not careful   b) intelligent   c) cheerful

_____ 35. **furious**   a) helpful   b) angry   c) quiet

_____ 36. **respect**   a) a great happiness   b) a great anger   c) a great liking

_____ 37. **sensitive**   a) not caring   b) understanding   c) happy

_____ 38. **wonder**   a) to answer   b) to blame   c) to want to know

_____ 39. **ignore**   a) to pay no attention to   b) to need   c) to know

_____ 40. **loyal**   a) mean   b) helpful   c) faithful

_____ 41. **tradition**   a) a fight   b) a handed-down way of doing something
c) a difficult time

_____ 42. **allow**   a) to let   b) to hate   c) to stop

_____ 43. **comfortable**   a) thirsty   b) relaxed   c) mean

_____ 44. **distract**   a) to take away attention   b) to make clean
c) to have questions about

_____ 45. **insulting**   a) easy to understand   b) hurtful   c) kind

_____ 46. **observe**   a) to miss   b) to watch   c) to copy

_____ 47. **opportunity**   a) a chance   b) a habit   c) a problem

_____ 48. **resist**   a) to say no to   b) to invite   c) to answer

---

SCORE: (Number correct _____ × 2) + 4 = _____ %

Unit 3: *Pretest*

In the space provided, write the letter of the choice that is closest in meaning to the **boldfaced** word.

_____ 1. **amazed**   **a**) surprised   **b**) bored   **c**) worried

_____ 2. **confident**   **a**) sorry   **b**) honest   **c**) sure

_____ 3. **donate**   **a**) to show   **b**) to find   **c**) to give

_____ 4. **effort**   **a**) hard work   **b**) sadness   **c**) good looks

_____ 5. **locate**   **a**) to lose   **b**) to find   **c**) to forget

_____ 6. **purpose**   **a**) a reason   **b**) a problem   **c**) a job

_____ 7. **sincere**   **a**) truthful   **b**) not honest   **c**) angry

_____ 8. **uncertain**   **a**) not interested   **b**) sure   **c**) not sure

_____ 9. **disgust**   **a**) make happy   **b**) make sick   **c**) make busy

_____ 10. **dismiss**   **a**) punish   **b**) forget   **c**) let leave

_____ 11. **guarantee**   **a**) a promise to fix something   **b**) a wish to go somewhere
          c) a hope to buy something

_____ 12. **ideal**   **a**) short   **b**) very bad   **c**) perfect

_____ 13. **inspect**   **a**) to hide carefully   **b**) to look at carefully   **c**) to stop

_____ 14. **opinion**   **a**) a thought   **b**) a need   **c**) a job

_____ 15. **prevent**   **a**) to stop ahead of time   **b**) to help   **c**) to cause

_____ 16. **resolve**   **a**) to forget   **b**) to fail   **c**) to decide

_____ 17. **advice**   **a**) a helpful idea   **b**) a friendship   **c**) a mistake

_____ 18. **cautious**   **a**) happy   **b**) tired   **c**) careful

_____ 19. **defeat**   **a**) to beat in a contest   **b**) to keep   **c**) to hide

_____ 20. **defect**   **a**) a cost   **b**) something wrong   **c**) the best part

_____ 21. **impossible**   **a**) usual   **b**) not able to happen   **c**) safe

_____ 22. **necessary**   **a**) not wanted   **b**) careful   **c**) very important

_____ 23. **permit**   **a**) to understand   **b**) to let   **c**) to win

_____ 24. **provide**   **a**) to give   **b**) to take away   **c**) to show

_____ 25. **arrange**   **a)** to buy   **b)** to mix up   **c)** to put in order

_____ 26. **continue**   **a)** to keep quiet   **b)** to keep outside   **c)** to keep going

_____ 27. **expert**   **a)** a person who does not know much about something   **b)** a person who knows a lot about something   **c)** a person who is afraid of something

_____ 28. **hollow**   **a)** against the law   **b)** out of shape   **c)** empty

_____ 29. **panic**   **a)** great fear   **b)** great hunger   **c)** great love

_____ 30. **personal**   **a)** not important   **b)** close to one's heart   **c)** not expensive

_____ 31. **regret**   **a)** to feel bad about   **b)** to be thankful   **c)** to be nervous

_____ 32. **suppose**   **a)** to remember   **b)** to see clearly   **c)** to guess

_____ 33. **admit**   **a)** to hide   **b)** to enjoy   **c)** to tell the truth

_____ 34. **available**   **a)** boring   **b)** easy to get   **c)** expensive

_____ 35. **contribute**   **a)** to give   **b)** to take away   **c)** to find

_____ 36. **dull**   **a)** not interesting   **b)** fun   **c)** private

_____ 37. **encourage**   **a)** to stop   **b)** to shout at angrily   **c)** to give hope to

_____ 38. **experiment**   **a)** to give   **b)** to try something new   **c)** to watch

_____ 39. **intimate**   **a)** boring   **b)** private   **c)** false

_____ 40. **portion**   **a)** all of something   **b)** nothing   **c)** a part of something

_____ 41. **compete**   **a)** to try to win   **b)** to give up   **c)** to share

_____ 42. **contain**   **a)** to dislike   **b)** to make   **c)** to have inside

_____ 43. **depend**   **a)** to wait for   **b)** to rely on   **c)** to turn away from

_____ 44. **effective**   **a)** late   **b)** slow   **c)** good

_____ 45. **envy**   **a)** to look like   **b)** to have more than   **c)** to want to have the same as

_____ 46. **gradual**   **a)** happening slowly   **b)** becoming smaller   **c)** happening quickly

_____ 47. **intense**   **a)** little   **b)** not important   **c)** deeply felt

_____ 48. **involve**   **a)** to keep out   **b)** to bring in   **c)** to make angry

---

SCORE: (Number correct _____ × 2) + 4 = _____ %

Unit 3: *Posttest*

In the space provided, write the letter of the choice that is closest in meaning to the **boldfaced** word.

_____ 1. **guarantee**   a) a hope to buy something   b) a wish to go somewhere
c) a promise to fix something

_____ 2. **ideal**   a) short   b) perfect   c) very bad

_____ 3. **inspect**   a) to look at carefully   b) to hide carefully   c) to stop

_____ 4. **opinion**   a) a need   b) a thought   c) a job

_____ 5. **prevent**   a) to help   b) to stop ahead of time   c) to cause

_____ 6. **resolve**   a) to decide   b) to fail   c) to forget

_____ 7. **advice**   a) a mistake   b) a friendship   c) a helpful idea

_____ 8. **cautious**   a) careful   b) tired   c) happy

_____ 9. **defeat**   a) to keep   b) to beat in a contest   c) to hide

_____ 10. **defect**   a) something wrong   b) a cost   c) the best part

_____ 11. **amazed**   a) worried   b) bored   c) surprised

_____ 12. **confident**   a) sorry   b) sure   c) honest

_____ 13. **donate**   a) to give   b) to find   c) to show

_____ 14. **effort**   a) good looks   b) sadness   c) hard work

_____ 15. **locate**   a) to find   b) to lose   c) to forget

_____ 16. **purpose**   a) a problem   b) a reason   c) a job

_____ 17. **sincere**   a) angry   b) not honest   c) truthful

_____ 18. **uncertain**   a) not sure   b) not interested   c) sure

_____ 19. **disgust**   a) make happy   b) make busy   c) make sick

_____ 20. **dismiss**   a) let leave   b) forget   c) punish

_____ 21. **compete**   a) to give up   b) to try to win   c) to share

_____ 22. **contain**   a) to have inside   b) to make   c) to dislike

_____ 23. **depend**   a) to rely on   b) to wait for   c) to turn away from

_____ 24. **effective**   a) slow   b) late   c) good

(Continues on next page)

_____ 25. **contribute**   **a**) to take away   **b**) to give   **c**) to find

_____ 26. **dull**   **a**) private   **b**) not interesting   **c**) fun

_____ 27. **encourage**   **a**) to give hope to   **b**) to stop   **c**) to shout at angrily

_____ 28. **experiment**   **a**) to give   **b**) to watch   **c**) to try something new

_____ 29. **admit**   **a**) to hide   **b**) to tell the truth   **c**) to enjoy

_____ 30. **available**   **a**) easy to get   **b**) boring   **c**) expensive

_____ 31. **envy**   **a**) to have more than   **b**) to want to have the same as   **c**) to look like

_____ 32. **gradual**   **a**) happening quickly   **b**) becoming smaller   **c**) happening slowly

_____ 33. **intense**   **a**) little   **b**) deeply felt   **c**) not important

_____ 34. **involve**   **a**) to bring in   **b**) to keep out   **c**) to make angry

_____ 35. **panic**   **a**) great love   **b**) great hunger   **c**) great fear

_____ 36. **personal**   **a**) not important   **b**) not expensive   **c**) close to one's heart

_____ 37. **regret**   **a**) to be thankful   **b**) to feel bad about   **c**) to be nervous

_____ 38. **suppose**   **a**) to guess   **b**) to see clearly   **c**) to remember

_____ 39. **intimate**   **a**) boring   **b**) false   **c**) private

_____ 40. **portion**   **a**) a part of something   **b**) nothing   **c**) all of something

_____ 41. **impossible**   **a**) safe   **b**) not able to happen   **c**) usual

_____ 42. **necessary**   **a**) very important   **b**) careful   **c**) not wanted

_____ 43. **permit**   **a**) to understand   **b**) to win   **c**) to let

_____ 44. **provide**   **a**) to take away   **b**) to give   **c**) to show

_____ 45. **arrange**   **a**) to mix up   **b**) to put in order   **c**) to buy

_____ 46. **continue**   **a**) to keep going   **b**) to keep outside   **c**) to keep quiet

_____ 47. **expert**   **a**) a person who does not know much about something   **b**) a person who is afraid of something   **c**) a person who knows a lot about something

_____ 48. **hollow**   **a**) out of shape   **b**) empty   **c**) against the law

_____

SCORE: (Number correct _____ × 2) + 4 = _____ %

In the space provided, write the letter of the choice that is closest in meaning to the **boldfaced** word.

_____ 1. **alarm**   **a)** to scare   **b)** to please   **c)** to relax

_____ 2. **collapse**   **a)** to build   **b)** to stay safe   **c)** to fall down

_____ 3. **defend**   **a)** to give up   **b)** to keep safe   **c)** to hurt

_____ 4. **grief**   **a)** sadness   **b)** happiness   **c)** boredom

_____ 5. **modest**   **a)** not working hard at something   **b)** not thinking too highly of oneself
     c) thinking very highly of oneself

_____ 6. **relieved**   **a)** unhappy   **b)** not caring   **c)** less worried

_____ 7. **similar**   **a)** not safe   **b)** good-looking   **c)** alike

_____ 8. **victim**   **a)** a person who is hurt   **b)** a person who hurts someone else
     c) a person who helps others

_____ 9. **confusion**   **a)** a feeling of danger   **b)** a feeling of not knowing what to do
     c) a feeling of peace

_____ 10. **decrease**   **a)** to make less   **b)** to make greater   **c)** to keep the same

_____ 11. **distant**   **a)** nearby   **b)** far away   **c)** different

_____ 12. **emerge**   **a)** to stay still   **b)** to get lost   **c)** to come out

_____ 13. **incident**   **a)** a time of trouble   **b)** a time of happiness   **c)** a time of resting

_____ 14. **realize**   **a)** to hope   **b)** to know   **c)** to write

_____ 15. **refuse**   **a)** to decide not to   **b)** to forget about   **c)** to want to

_____ 16. **survive**   **a)** to live through   **b)** to forget   **c)** to cause

_____ 17. **excess**   **a)** used   **b)** good   **c)** extra

_____ 18. **persuade**   **a)** to get someone to do something   **b)** to stop   **c)** to leave

_____ 19. **quarrel**   **a)** a reason   **b)** a fight   **c)** a dream

_____ 20. **reaction**   **a)** something that happens because of something else   **b)** an action that
is hard to do   **c)** more of something than is needed

_____ 21. **reveal**   **a)** to hide   **b)** to forget   **c)** to tell

_____ 22. **separate**   **a)** to bring together   **b)** to make larger   **c)** to put in different places

_____ 23. **stubborn**   **a)** easy to get along with   **b)** not wanting to do something
     c) quick to learn

_____ 24. **tremendous**   **a)** friendly   **b)** ugly   **c)** big

(Continues on next page)

_____ 25. **disaster**   **a**) something that causes suffering   **b**) something interesting
    c) something that turns out well

_____ 26. **fascinate**   **a**) to bore greatly   **b**) to frighten   **c**) to interest greatly

_____ 27. **generous**   **a**) willing to share   **b**) selfish   **c**) bad-tempered

_____ 28. **increase**   **a**) to make smaller   **b**) to make greater   **c**) to get rid of

_____ 29. **predict**   **a**) to lie   **b**) to tell ahead of time   **c**) to forget

_____ 30. **progress**   **a**) mistakes   **b**) friends   **c**) movement toward a goal

_____ 31. **scarce**   **a**) easily found   **b**) famous   **c**) few in number

_____ 32. **tolerate**   **a**) to let happen   **b**) to stop   **c**) to hide

_____ 33. **detail**   **a**) the end   **b**) a small part   **c**) a color

_____ 34. **glare**   **a**) to choose   **b**) to smile   **c**) to look at in an angry way

_____ 35. **humor**   **a**) a lesson   **b**) anger   **c**) something funny

_____ 36. **notice**   **a**) to see   **b**) to forget   **c**) to choose

_____ 37. **occupy**   **a**) to break   **b**) to clean   **c**) to live in

_____ 38. **perform**   **a**) to do   **b**) to fail   **c**) to leave

_____ 39. **select**   **a**) to break   **b**) to lose   **c**) to choose

_____ 40. **weary**   **a**) sad   **b**) wide awake   **c**) tired

_____ 41. **condemn**   **a**) to help   **b**) to speak strongly against   **c**) to give thanks for

_____ 42. **embrace**   **a**) to speak in an angry way   **b**) to make fun of   **c**) to hug

_____ 43. **express**   **a**) to make feelings known   **b**) to whisper   **c**) to picture in one's mind

_____ 44. **familiar**   **a**) far away   **b**) well-known   **c**) sad

_____ 45. **imagine**   **a**) to picture in the mind   **b**) to forget   **c**) to say something nice

_____ 46. **isolate**   **a**) to put into a group with everyone else   **b**) to teach
    c) to put by oneself

_____ 47. **support**   **a**) to show caring for   **b**) to blame   **c**) to meet

_____ 48. **unite**   **a**) to join together   **b**) to fight   **c**) to keep alone

---

SCORE: (Number correct _____ × 2) + 4 = _____ %

Name: _____

Unit 4: *Posttest*

In the space provided, write the letter of the choice that is closest in meaning to the **boldfaced** word.

_____ 1. **condemn**   **a)** to speak strongly against   **b)** to help   **c)** to give thanks for

_____ 2. **embrace**   **a)** to hug   **b)** to make fun of   **c)** to speak in an angry way

_____ 3. **express**   **a)** to picture in one's mind   **b)** to whisper   **c)** to make feelings known

_____ 4. **familiar**   **a)** well-known   **b)** far away   **c)** sad

_____ 5. **imagine**   **a)** to forget   **b)** to picture in the mind   **c)** to say something nice

_____ 6. **survive**   **a)** to cause   **b)** to forget   **c)** to live through

_____ 7. **excess**   **a)** extra   **b)** good   **c)** used

_____ 8. **persuade**   **a)** to stop   **b)** to get someone to do something   **c)** to leave

_____ 9. **quarrel**   **a)** a fight   **b)** a reason   **c)** a dream

_____ 10. **reaction**   **a)** an action that is hard to do   **b)** more of something than is needed
     c) something that happens because of something else

_____ 11. **reveal**   **a)** to hide   **b)** to tell   **c)** to forget

_____ 12. **separate**   **a)** to put in different places   **b)** to make larger   **c)** to bring together

_____ 13. **stubborn**   **a)** easy to get along with   **b)** quick to learn
     c) not wanting to do something

_____ 14. **tremendous**   **a)** friendly   **b)** big   **c)** ugly

_____ 15. **disaster**   **a)** something that turns out well   **b)** something interesting
     c) something that causes suffering

_____ 16. **fascinate**   **a)** to interest greatly   **b)** to frighten   **c)** to bore greatly

_____ 17. **generous**   **a)** selfish   **b)** willing to share   **c)** bad-tempered

_____ 18. **increase**   **a)** to make greater   **b)** to get rid of   **c)** to make smaller

_____ 19. **predict**   **a)** to lie   **b)** to tell ahead of time   **c)** to forget

_____ 20. **progress**   **a)** mistakes   **b)** movement toward a goal   **c)** friends

_____ 21. **distant**   **a)** far away   **b)** nearby   **c)** different

_____ 22. **emerge**   **a)** to stay still   **b)** to come out   **c)** to get lost

_____ 23. **incident**   **a)** a time of resting   **b)** a time of happiness   **c)** a time of trouble

_____ 24. **realize**   **a)** to hope   **b)** to write   **c)** to know

(Continues on next page)

_____ 25. **refuse**   **a)** to want to   **b)** to decide not to   **c)** to forget about

_____ 26. **relieved**   **a)** less worried   **b)** not caring   **c)** unhappy

_____ 27. **similar**   **a)** alike   **b)** good-looking   **c)** not safe

_____ 28. **victim**   **a)** a person who hurts someone else   **b)** a person who is hurt
c) a person who helps others

_____ 29. **confusion**   **a)** a feeling of peace   **b)** a feeling of not knowing what to do
c) a feeling of danger

_____ 30. **decrease**   **a)** to make greater   **b)** to make less   **c)** to keep the same

_____ 31. **scarce**   **a)** famous   **b)** easily found   **c)** few in number

_____ 32. **tolerate**   **a)** to hide   **b)** to stop   **c)** to let happen

_____ 33. **detail**   **a)** a small part   **b)** a color   **c)** the end

_____ 34. **glare**   **a)** to choose   **b)** to look at in an angry way   **c)** to smile

_____ 35. **humor**   **a)** something funny   **b)** anger   **c)** a lesson

_____ 36. **isolate**   **a)** to put into a group with everyone else   **b)** to put by oneself
c) to teach

_____ 37. **support**   **a)** to meet   **b)** to blame   **c)** to show caring for

_____ 38. **unite**   **a)** to fight   **b)** to join together   **c)** to keep alone

_____ 39. **select**   **a)** to break   **b)** to choose   **c)** to lose

_____ 40. **weary**   **a)** tired   **b)** wide awake   **c)** sad

_____ 41. **alarm**   **a)** to please   **b)** to scare   **c)** to relax

_____ 42. **collapse**   **a)** to stay safe   **b)** to fall down   **c)** to build

_____ 43. **defend**   **a)** to keep safe   **b)** to hurt   **c)** to give up

_____ 44. **grief**   **a)** happiness   **b)** sadness   **c)** boredom

_____ 45. **modest**   **a)** not working hard at something   **b)** thinking very highly of oneself
c) not thinking too highly of oneself

_____ 46. **notice**   **a)** to forget   **b)** to see   **c)** to choose

_____ 47. **occupy**   **a)** to live in   **b)** to clean   **c)** to break

_____ 48. **perform**   **a)** to fail   **b)** to do   **c)** to leave

SCORE: (Number correct _____ × 2) + 4 = _____ %

Name: _____

Unit 5: *Pretest*

In the space provided, write the letter of the choice that is closest in meaning to the **boldfaced** word.

_____ 1. **admire**   **a)** to laugh at   **b)** to think highly of   **c)** to forget

_____ 2. **bold**   **a)** afraid   **b)** cruel   **c)** brave

_____ 3. **comment**   **a)** something that is said or written   **b)** a wrong answer   **c)** a law

_____ 4. **develop**   **a)** to grow a little at a time   **b)** to leave   **c)** to dry

_____ 5. **expect**   **a)** to dislike   **b)** to want   **c)** to believe something will happen

_____ 6. **insist**   **a)** to make believe   **b)** to get close to someone   **c)** to say very strongly

_____ 7. **pretend**   **a)** to make believe   **b)** to grow   **c)** to know

_____ 8. **solution**   **a)** a reason for doing something   **b)** a question   **c)** an answer to a problem

_____ 9. **appear**   **a)** to seem   **b)** to think   **c)** to dislike

_____ 10. **attract**   **a)** to scare off   **b)** to make angry   **c)** to cause to come near

_____ 11. **common**   **a)** very large   **b)** strange   **c)** happening often

_____ 12. **conceal**   **a)** to bother   **b)** to make sad   **c)** to hide

_____ 13. **enormous**   **a)** very small   **b)** very large   **c)** very good-looking

_____ 14. **irritate**   **a)** to help   **b)** to calm down   **c)** to bother

_____ 15. **mention**   **a)** to talk about   **b)** to forget about   **c)** to think about

_____ 16. **surround**   **a)** to make happy   **b)** to be on all sides of   **c)** to move away from

_____ 17. **achieve**   **a)** to lose   **b)** to have trouble with   **c)** to reach a goal

_____ 18. **condition**   **a)** the shape something is in   **b)** a neighborhood   **c)** news

_____ 19. **duty**   **a)** a job   **b)** a hobby   **c)** a problem

_____ 20. **exhaust**   **a)** to make happy   **b)** to make strong   **c)** to make tired

_____ 21. **injury**   **a)** a movement   **b)** harm   **c)** good health

_____ 22. **major**   **a)** small   **b)** not expensive   **c)** big

_____ 23. **seldom**   **a)** every day   **b)** not often   **c)** on purpose

_____ 24. **value**   **a)** a reason   **b)** a color   **c)** what something is worth

(Continues on next page)

_____ 25. **advance**   **a)** to stop moving   **b)** to move forward   **c)** to move away

_____ 26. **consider**   **a)** to cover up   **b)** to think about   **c)** to want

_____ 27. **delicate**   **a)** good to eat   **b)** strong   **c)** easily broken

_____ 28. **grasp**   **a)** to grab   **b)** to slap   **c)** to drop

_____ 29. **interrupt**   **a)** to calm   **b)** to help   **c)** to stop for a short time

_____ 30. **praise**   **a)** to leave alone   **b)** to dislike   **c)** to say good things about

_____ 31. **request**   **a)** a problem   **b)** an answer   **c)** something that is asked for

_____ 32. **succeed**   **a)** to do badly   **b)** to do well   **c)** to pay too much

_____ 33. **attempt**   **a)** to repeat   **b)** to try   **c)** to remember

_____ 34. **courteous**   **a)** silly   **b)** frightened   **c)** polite

_____ 35. **explore**   **a)** to travel around   **b)** to lose   **c)** to be afraid of

_____ 36. **hopeless**   **a)** happy   **b)** without hope   **c)** tired

_____ 37. **imitate**   **a)** to see   **b)** to hide   **c)** to copy

_____ 38. **permanent**   **a)** good   **b)** new   **c)** long-lasting

_____ 39. **recognize**   **a)** to know from before   **b)** to study   **c)** to lose

_____ 40. **sufficient**   **a)** expensive   **b)** too much   **c)** enough

_____ 41. **assist**   **a)** to find   **b)** to look at carefully   **c)** to help

_____ 42. **competent**   **a)** dangerous   **b)** good at something   **c)** boring

_____ 43. **enemy**   **a)** someone who is perfect   **b)** someone who is liked
c) someone who is hated

_____ 44. **examine**   **a)** to leave   **b)** to use   **c)** to look at carefully

_____ 45. **flaw**   **a)** something wrong   **b)** a good part   **c)** good looks

_____ 46. **positive**   **a)** sad   **b)** healthy   **c)** hopeful

_____ 47. **sample**   **a)** a picture   **b)** a small amount   **c)** a sale

_____ 48. **urge**   **a)** a strong dislike   **b)** a great fear   **c)** a strong wish

---

SCORE: (Number correct _____ × 2) + 4 = _____ %

Name: _____

Unit 5: *Posttest*

In the space provided, write the letter of the choice that is closest in meaning to the **boldfaced** word.

_____ 1. **assist** **a)** to help **b)** to look at carefully **c)** to find

_____ 2. **competent** **a)** dangerous **b)** boring **c)** good at something

_____ 3. **enemy** **a)** someone who is hated **b)** someone who is liked **c)** someone who is perfect

_____ 4. **examine** **a)** to use **b)** to look at carefully **c)** to leave

_____ 5. **advance** **a)** to move away **b)** to stop moving **c)** to move forward

_____ 6. **surround** **a)** to be on all sides of **b)** to move away from **c)** to make happy

_____ 7. **achieve** **a)** to have trouble with **b)** to reach a goal **c)** to lose

_____ 8. **condition** **a)** a neighborhood **b)** news **c)** the shape something is in

_____ 9. **duty** **a)** a hobby **b)** a job **c)** a problem

_____ 10. **exhaust** **a)** to make happy **b)** to make tired **c)** to make strong

_____ 11. **request** **a)** an answer **b)** something that is asked for **c)** a problem

_____ 12. **succeed** **a)** to do well **b)** to do badly **c)** to pay too much

_____ 13. **attempt** **a)** to repeat **b)** to remember **c)** to try

_____ 14. **courteous** **a)** polite **b)** frightened **c)** silly

_____ 15. **explore** **a)** to be afraid of **b)** to lose **c)** to travel around

_____ 16. **insist** **a)** to make believe **b)** to say very strongly **c)** to get close to someone

_____ 17. **pretend** **a)** to know **b)** to grow **c)** to make believe

_____ 18. **solution** **a)** a reason for doing something **b)** an answer to a problem **c)** a question

_____ 19. **appear** **a)** to think **b)** to seem **c)** to dislike

_____ 20. **attract** **a)** to cause to come near **b)** to make angry **c)** to scare off

_____ 21. **common** **a)** happening often **b)** strange **c)** very large

_____ 22. **conceal** **a)** to bother **b)** to hide **c)** to make sad

_____ 23. **enormous** **a)** very large **b)** very small **c)** very good-looking

_____ 24. **irritate** **a)** to help **b)** to calm down **c)** to bother

(Continues on next page)

_____ 25. **mention** **a)** to think about **b)** to forget about **c)** to talk about

_____ 26. **hopeless** **a)** tired **b)** without hope **c)** happy

_____ 27. **imitate** **a)** to copy **b)** to hide **c)** to see

_____ 28. **permanent** **a)** good **b)** long-lasting **c)** new

_____ 29. **recognize** **a)** to lose **b)** to know from before **c)** to study

_____ 30. **sufficient** **a)** enough **b)** too much **c)** expensive

_____ 31. **admire** **a)** to laugh at **b)** to forget **c)** to think highly of

_____ 32. **bold** **a)** afraid **b)** brave **c)** cruel

_____ 33. **comment** **a)** a wrong answer **b)** something that is said or written **c)** a law

_____ 34. **develop** **a)** to dry **b)** to leave **c)** to grow a little at a time

_____ 35. **flaw** **a)** a good part **b)** good looks **c)** something wrong

_____ 36. **positive** **a)** hopeful **b)** healthy **c)** sad

_____ 37. **sample** **a)** a small amount **b)** a picture **c)** a sale

_____ 38. **urge** **a)** a strong wish **b)** a great fear **c)** a strong dislike

_____ 39. **interrupt** **a)** to calm **b)** to stop for a short time **c)** to help

_____ 40. **praise** **a)** to say good things about **b)** to dislike **c)** to leave alone

_____ 41. **injury** **a)** a movement **b)** good health **c)** harm

_____ 42. **major** **a)** small **b)** big **c)** not expensive

_____ 43. **seldom** **a)** not often **b)** on purpose **c)** every day

_____ 44. **value** **a)** a reason **b)** what something is worth **c)** a color

_____ 45. **expect** **a)** to believe something will happen **b)** to want **c)** to dislike

_____ 46. **consider** **a)** to cover up **b)** to want **c)** to think about

_____ 47. **delicate** **a)** easily broken **b)** strong **c)** good to eat

_____ 48. **grasp** **a)** to slap **b)** to grab **c)** to drop

SCORE: (Number correct _____ × 2) + 4 = _____ %

Pretest / Posttest

ANSWER SHEET

1. ____	26. ____	51. ____	76. ____
2. ____	27. ____	52. ____	77. ____
3. ____	28. ____	53. ____	78. ____
4. ____	29. ____	54. ____	79. ____
5. ____	30. ____	55. ____	80. ____
6. ____	31. ____	56. ____	81. ____
7. ____	32. ____	57. ____	82. ____
8. ____	33. ____	58. ____	83. ____
9. ____	34. ____	59. ____	84. ____
10. ____	35. ____	60. ____	85. ____
11. ____	36. ____	61. ____	86. ____
12. ____	37. ____	62. ____	87. ____
13. ____	38. ____	63. ____	88. ____
14. ____	39. ____	64. ____	89. ____
15. ____	40. ____	65. ____	90. ____
16. ____	41. ____	66. ____	91. ____
17. ____	42. ____	67. ____	92. ____
18. ____	43. ____	68. ____	93. ____
19. ____	44. ____	69. ____	94. ____
20. ____	45. ____	70. ____	95. ____
21. ____	46. ____	71. ____	96. ____
22. ____	47. ____	72. ____	97. ____
23. ____	48. ____	73. ____	98. ____
24. ____	49. ____	74. ____	99. ____
25. ____	50. ____	75. ____	100. ____

ANSWER KEY

1. c	26. a	51. a	76. b
2. c	27. b	52. b	77. a
3. a	28. a	53. c	78. c
4. c	29. b	54. c	79. b
5. c	30. c	55. b	80. c
6. b	31. c	56. c	81. c
7. c	32. a	57. c	82. a
8. a	33. c	58. c	83. a
9. c	34. c	59. a	84. a
10. c	35. c	60. c	85. a
11. a	36. b	61. c	86. c
12. b	37. c	62. c	87. b
13. a	38. a	63. c	88. c
14. a	39. b	64. b	89. b
15. c	40. b	65. b	90. c
16. a	41. c	66. a	91. b
17. b	42. c	67. c	92. c
18. a	43. b	68. b	93. a
19. c	44. a	69. b	94. c
20. b	45. b	70. c	95. b
21. b	46. c	71. a	96. b
22. b	47. a	72. c	97. b
23. a	48. a	73. c	98. b
24. b	49. a	74. a	99. c
25. c	50. c	75. b	100. c

ANSWER KEY

1. c	26. c	51. a	76. a
2. c	27. b	52. c	77. c
3. b	28. a	53. a	78. a
4. c	29. c	54. c	79. b
5. b	30. b	55. a	80. a
6. a	31. c	56. b	81. b
7. b	32. a	57. b	82. a
8. a	33. c	58. b	83. b
9. c	34. a	59. a	84. a
10. b	35. c	60. a	85. b
11. a	36. a	61. b	86. a
12. c	37. b	62. a	87. a
13. b	38. c	63. b	88. b
14. b	39. b	64. a	89. c
15. c	40. b	65. c	90. b
16. b	41. b	66. c	91. c
17. c	42. b	67. b	92. b
18. c	43. a	68. c	93. a
19. b	44. b	69. b	94. b
20. c	45. c	70. a	95. a
21. a	46. a	71. a	96. c
22. c	47. b	72. b	97. a
23. a	48. b	73. c	98. c
24. b	49. c	74. b	99. a
25. a	50. a	75. b	100. c

Answers to the Unit Pretests and Posttests:
VOCABULARY BASICS

	Unit One		Unit Two		Unit Three		Unit Four		Unit Five	
	Pretest	Posttest	Pretest	Posttest	Pretest	Posttest	Pretest	Posttest	Pretest	Posttest
1.	c	b	c	b	a	c	a	a	b	a
2.	b	c	a	c	c	b	c	a	c	c
3.	c	c	b	c	c	a	b	c	a	a
4.	b	b	c	b	a	b	a	a	a	b
5.	a	a	b	a	b	b	b	b	c	c
6.	a	b	a	b	a	a	c	c	c	a
7.	a	b	b	a	a	c	c	a	a	b
8.	c	a	c	a	c	a	a	b	c	c
9.	a	c	b	b	b	b	b	a	a	b
10.	c	b	b	a	c	a	a	c	c	b
11.	b	a	c	c	a	c	b	b	c	b
12.	c	b	c	c	c	b	c	a	c	a
13.	b	a	a	b	b	a	a	c	b	c
14.	c	b	b	c	a	c	b	b	c	a
15.	a	b	c	a	a	a	a	c	a	c
16.	c	b	c	b	a	b	a	a	b	b
17.	b	a	b	a	c	c	c	b	c	c
18.	a	c	a	a	c	a	a	a	a	b
19.	a	b	b	c	a	c	b	b	a	b
20.	c	c	c	c	b	a	a	b	c	a
21.	b	b	c	a	b	b	c	a	b	a
22.	c	a	a	b	c	a	c	b	c	b
23.	b	b	b	c	b	a	b	c	b	a
24.	c	c	c	c	a	c	c	c	c	c
25.	b	b	c	a	c	b	a	b	b	c
26.	a	b	b	a	c	b	c	a	b	b
27.	c	a	b	b	b	a	a	a	c	a
28.	c	b	a	c	c	c	b	b	a	b
29.	c	c	c	a	a	b	b	b	c	b
30.	a	b	b	c	b	a	c	b	c	a
31.	c	b	c	b	a	b	c	c	c	c
32.	a	c	a	b	c	c	a	c	b	b
33.	a	b	a	c	c	b	b	a	b	b
34.	c	b	b	a	b	a	c	b	c	c
35.	a	a	c	b	a	c	c	a	a	c
36.	b	c	c	c	a	c	a	b	b	a
37.	c	c	c	b	c	b	c	c	c	a
38.	c	b	b	c	b	a	a	b	c	a
39.	a	c	c	a	b	c	c	b	a	b
40.	c	a	a	c	c	a	c	a	c	a
41.	a	b	b	b	a	b	b	b	c	c
42.	c	b	a	a	c	a	c	b	b	b
43.	b	c	c	b	b	c	a	a	c	a
44.	a	b	c	a	c	b	b	b	c	b
45.	b	a	b	b	c	b	a	c	a	a
46.	c	b	b	b	a	a	c	b	c	c
47.	a	a	c	a	c	c	a	a	b	a
48.	c	c	a	a	b	b	a	b	c	b

44

Mastery Test: *Chapter 1 (The Nose Knows; Barbie)*

PART A. Using the answer line, complete each item below with the correct word from the box.

a. **curious**	c. **odor**
b. **fact**	d. **suggest**

_____ 1. It is a . . ? . . that too much sun is bad for your skin.

_____ 2. Since you enjoy writing, I . . ? . . that you work on the school newspaper.

_____ 3. We opened all the windows to get rid of the . . ? . . of cigarettes.

_____ 4. The little boy was . . ? . . about what was inside his birthday present.

PART B. Using the answer line, complete each item below with the correct word from the box.

e. **agreement**	g. **flexible**
f. **cancel**	h. **prepare**

_____ 5. Uncooked spaghetti is stiff, but after it has been cooked, it is . . ? . . .

_____ 6. If the band doesn't show up, we will have to . . ? . . the concert.

_____ 7. Since my mother and I always argue about politics, we've made an . . ? . . not to talk about the subject.

_____ 8. Students . . ? . . for a test by studying.

SCORE: (Number correct) _____ × 12.5 = _____ %

Name: _____

Mastery Test: *Chapter 2 (Feeling Blue; A Late Love Letter)*

PART A. Using the answer line, complete each item below with the correct word from the box.

a. **entertains**	c. **produced**
b. **experience**	d. **tension**

_____ 1. From a few potatoes, carrots, an onion and some broth, Emily . . ? . . a delicious soup.

_____ 2. Babies love to have a mirror hanging in their crib. It . . ? . . them to stare at their own faces.

_____ 3. A headache can be caused by . . ? . ., because your muscles tighten up when you're nervous or upset.

_____ 4. When her teacher asked her to write a paper about a happy . . ? . ., Jada wrote about the time she visited her favorite aunt and uncle.

PART B. Using the answer line, complete each item below with the correct word from the box.

e. **daily**	g. **negative**
f. **identify**	h. **original**

_____ 5. Politicians say too many . . ? . . things about each other. Don't you get tired of hearing them say such mean things?

_____ 6. I don't always eat the right foods, so I take a . . ? . . vitamin pill to help keep me healthy.

_____ 7. Because the baby was dressed all in pink, I could . . ? . . her as a girl.

_____ 8. Instead of just singing "Happy Birthday" at Dad's party, we made up an . . ? . . birthday song for him.

SCORE: (Number correct) _____ × 12.5 = _____ %

Name: _____

Mastery Test: *Chapter 3 (Ads That Lie; Horrible Hiccups)*

PART A. Using the answer line, complete each item below with the correct word from the box.

a. **conclusion**	c. **protect**
b. **event**	d. **talent**

_____ 1. Bring your bike into the garage to . . ? . . it from the rain.

_____ 2. Moving to a new home is a big . . ? . . in anyone's life.

_____ 3. Dessert is usually served at the . . ? . . of a meal.

_____ 4. When my oven stopped working, I called a friend who has a . . ? . . for fixing things.

PART B. Using the answer line, complete each item below with the correct word from the box.

e. **attack**	g. **minor**
f. **humble**	h. **volunteer**

_____ 5. Although Mrs. Clark is . . ? . . about her own success, she is proud of her children's successes.

_____ 6. If you put a small fish in a tank with a larger fish, the larger fish may . . ? . . it and eat it.

_____ 7. The two children get along very well. They have . . ? . . disagreements once in a while, but they never really fight.

_____ 8. The teacher asked for a . . ? . . to help clean the classroom before Parents' Night.

SCORE: (Number correct) _____ × 12.5 = _____ %

Name: _____

Mastery Test: *Chapter 4 (An Upsetting Dream; A King's Mistake)*

PART A. Using the answer line, complete each item below with the correct word from the box.

a. **claims**	c. **inspired**
b. **embarrassed**	d. **unusual**

_____ 1. A news program about homeless people . . ? . . Shawn to collect food for people living on the street.

_____ 2. The rock star gave his daughter an . . ? . . name: Moon Unit.

_____ 3. I was . . ? . . when I called a friend, then forgot her name as soon as she answered.

_____ 4. A woman in Alabama . . ? . . to be the oldest living American.

PART B. Using the answer line, complete each item below with the correct word from the box.

e. **accused**	g. **precious**
f. **pleasant**	h. **public**

_____ 5. My photograph album is . . ? . . to me. I wouldn't sell it for any amount of money.

_____ 6. The neighbors argue all the time. This week, one of them . . ? . . the other of stealing the newspaper off her porch.

_____ 7. Most meetings of the school board are . . ? . . —that is, any one can attend them.

_____ 8. I liked my brother's girlfriend right away. She has such a sweet, . . ? . . face.

SCORE: (Number correct) _____ × 12.5 = _____ %

Name: _____

Mastery Test: *Chapter 5 (Be Proud of Age; Making Anger Work)*

PART A. Using the answer line, complete each item below with the correct word from the box.

a. **benefited**	c. **emphasized**
b. **delayed**	d. **logical**

_____ 1. Speaking very seriously, Dad . . ? . . that we were to be home before dark.

_____ 2. The small, sickly kitten quickly . . ? . . from a good home, good food, and lots of love.

_____ 3. It isn't . . ? . . to wear shorts today—it's really cold outside.

_____ 4. The flight to Chicago was . . ? . . because of heavy fog.

PART B. Using the answer line, complete each item below with the correct word from the box.

e. **rivals**	g. **tempt**
f. **satisfy**	h. **vacant**

_____ 5. Jim quit smoking a year ago, but cigarettes still . . ? . . him. He says he wants one every day.

_____ 6. Barb and Tonya have become . . ? . . in science class. Both are good students, and both want to get the highest grade in class.

_____ 7. I'll probably never meet my favorite movie star, so watching his movies will have to . . ? . . my wish to see him.

_____ 8. Since my dog died, it makes me sad to see his . . ? . . doghouse in the back yard.

SCORE: (Number correct) _____ × 12.5 = _____ %

Mastery Test: *Chapter 6 (Customers; Stuck in the Middle)*

PART A. Using the answer line, complete each item below with the correct word from the box.

a. **definite**	c. **specific**
b. **motivated**	d. **suspect**

_____ 1. Sandra was . . ? . . to make friends with her co-worker when she learned that the co-worker had an attractive single brother.

_____ 2. Police . . ? . . that the department-store fire was set on purpose.

_____ 3. Is it . . ? . . that the party has been canceled, or is that just a rumor?

_____ 4. All the cartoons in the book are funny, but there is a . . ? . . one that makes me laugh especially hard.

PART B. Using the answer line, complete each item below with the correct word from the box.

e. **fortunate**	g. **oppose**
f. **leisure**	h. **refers**

_____ 5. Gayle is . . ? . . to have a job she likes very much that pays well, too.

_____ 6. Although their parents think it might be best, the twins . . ? . . the idea of being put into separate classes at school.

_____ 7. Sean jokingly . . ? . . to his wife as "the boss."

_____ 8. Our cats live a life of . . ? . . , napping many more hours than they are awake.

SCORE: (Number correct) _____ × 12.5 = _____ %

Name: _____

Mastery Test: *Chapter 7 (Joy of Ice Cream; A Noisy Apartment)*

PART A. Using the answer line, complete each item below with the correct word from the box.

a. **devour**	c. **occasions**
b. **modern**	d. **popular**

_____ 1. Every year there are some . . ? . . toys that many children want—things like virtual pets or "beanie babies."

_____ 2. During the winter, the birds quickly . . ? . . any seed we put in the birdfeeder.

_____ 3. Our favorite restaurant is rather expensive, so we go there only on special . . ? . . .

_____ 4. My parents listen to records they play on a turntable, while I play music on a more . . ? . . CD player.

PART B. Using the answer line, complete each item below with the correct word from the box.

e. **aware**	g. **discovered**
f. **constant**	h. **distressed**

_____ 5. Emily was . . ? . . to notice that the stone had fallen out of her ring.

_____ 6. The waiter came over with a pitcher of water when he became . . ? . . that our glasses were empty.

_____ 7. Wherever movie stars go, they hear the . . ? . . "click-click-click" of cameras going off.

_____ 8. The children screamed with joy when they . . ? . . their presents hidden behind the living-room couch.

SCORE: (Number correct) _____ × 12.5 = _____ %

VOCABULARY BASICS

Mastery Test: *Chapter 8 (Nuts in the Senate; Calling Dr. Leech)*

PART A. Using the answer line, complete each item below with the correct word from the box.

a. **created**	c. **glanced**
b. **failure**	d. **introduce**

_____ 1. The tired man just . . ? . . at the menu, then said, "Bring me whatever's on special tonight."

_____ 2. Martin wanted to . . ? . . himself to a girl at the dance, but he felt too shy.

_____ 3. The party was a dreadful . . ? . . Only half the invited guests showed up, and those that did just stood around looking bored.

_____ 4. Steven Spielberg has . . ? . . some of the most successful movies of all time, including *E.T., Jaws,* and *Jurassic Park.*

PART B. Using the answer line, complete each item below with the correct word from the box.

e. **ability**	g. **gratitude**
f. **damage**	h. **labor**

_____ 5. I think Isaac was born with the . . ? . . to draw—he's always been good at it.

_____ 6. Raking the leaves alone would have taken an hour, but I got it done in thirty minutes because a friend shared the . . ? . . .

_____ 7. The big dog raced through the house, knocking over vases and lamps and doing a lot of . . ? . . .

_____ 8. Sending a thank-you card is one way to express your . . ? . . .

SCORE: (Number correct) _____ × 12.5 = _____ %

Name: _____

Mastery Test: *Chapter 9 (TV and Violence; Ready for a Pet?)*

PART A. Using the answer line, complete each item below with the correct word from the box.

a. **avoid**	c. **includes**
b. **excuse**	d. **normal**

_____ 1. The boss did not believe Eric's . . ? . . for being late, which was, "I stopped to help an old lady cross a dangerous street."

_____ 2. People often . . ? . . other people they don't want to talk to.

_____ 3. We have two pet frogs. One is all white with pink eyes, while the other is the . . ? . . green color.

_____ 4. The art set . . ? . . colored pencils, watercolors, and a pad of paper.

PART B. Using the answer line, complete each item below with the correct word from the box.

e. **helpless**	g. **sociable**
f. **intended**	h. **struggle**

_____ 5. A turtle on its back is . . ? . . . It can do nothing but lie there and wave its legs around.

_____ 6. It is a . . ? . . to pay my bills out of my small paycheck.

_____ 7. Sarah . . ? . . to use coupons at the supermarket, but she accidentally left them at home.

_____ 8. Most puppies are quite . . ? . . , ready to make friends with anyone who comes near.

SCORE: (Number correct) _____ × 12.5 = _____ %

Mastery Test: *Chapter 10 (Help for Shy People; Laughing Matter)*

PART A. Using the answer line, complete each item below with the correct word from the box.

a. **damp**	c. **requires**
b. **numerous**	d. **timid**

_____ 1. John thought he wouldn't be scared when he met his favorite movie star, but when it happened he felt so . . ? . . that all he could say was "Hi!"

_____ 2. The boy's room contains . . ? . . pieces of sports equipment: a basketball, a baseball glove, a hockey stick, and roller blades.

_____ 3. When people are nervous, the palms of their hands often become . . ? . . .

_____ 4. Julia . . ? . . everyone who rides in her car to wear a seat belt.

PART B. Using the answer line, complete each item below with the correct word from the box.

e. **approached**	g. **loyal**
f. **ignore**	h. **previous**

_____ 5. When the telephone rang, I didn't know whether to answer it or . . ? . . it.

_____ 6. A woman in the store . . ? . . me and said, "Don't you remember who I am?"

_____ 7. We had pork chops on Tuesday, but I can't remember what we ate the . . ? . . evening.

_____ 8. Even when good friends disagree, they are still . . ? . . to one another.

SCORE: (Number correct) _____ × 12.5 = _____ %

Mastery Test: *Chapter 11 (Taking Risks; Bad Manners Hurt)*

PART A. Using the answer line, complete each item below with the correct word from the box.

a. **capable**	c. **opportunity**
b. **observes**	d. **resist**

_____ 1. Living with her Mexican grandmother gave Anna the . . ? . . to learn Spanish.

_____ 2. Stan took a bike repair course so he would be . . ? . . of fixing his own bike.

_____ 3. The store is full of people who can't . . ? . . a good sale.

_____ 4. Our dog . . ? . . us carefully as we eat dinner, hoping we will offer him a bite.

PART B. Using the answer line, complete each item below with the correct word from the box.

e. **careless**	g. **reversed**
f. **furious**	h. **tradition**

_____ 5. It was . . ? . . of you to leave that glass so close to the edge of the table. Didn't you realize it could spill?

_____ 6. I accidentally . . ? . . my shirt and wore it with the front in the back.

_____ 7. Does your family follow the . . ? . . of putting a child's tooth under the pillow for the Tooth Fairy to find?

_____ 8. Max became . . ? . . when his car broke down again just after he had paid to have it repaired.

SCORE: (Number correct) _____ × 12.5 = _____ %

Mastery Test: *Chapter 12 (Two Different Sisters; Honest Abe)*

PART A. Using the answer line, complete each item below with the correct word from the box.

a. **comfortable**	c. **insulting**
b. **distract**	d. **sensitive**

_____ 1. Do you like to study with music playing, or does the noise . . ? . . you?

_____ 2. It feels good to get out of high-heeled shoes and into a pair of . . ? . . sneakers.

_____ 3. A . . ? . . person cares about the feelings of those around him or her.

_____ 4. Because he was angry at her, George began . . ? . . Lisa about everything from her hair style to her choice of friends.

PART B. Using the answer line, complete each item below with the correct word from the box.

e. **allow**	g. **respect**
f. **persisted**	h. **wonder**

_____ 5. At what age do you think parents should . . ? . . their children to date?

_____ 6. Tom's . . ? . . for his coach is great. He listens carefully to his advice on all subjects.

_____ 7. I . . ? . . what would happen if I pushed that button that says "Do Not Touch."

_____ 8. The pushy waiter . . ? . . in asking us if we wanted dessert, even after we'd told him no twice.

SCORE: (Number correct) _____ × 12.5 = _____ %

Name: _____

Mastery Test: *Chapter 13 (Ready to Do Well; Advertising for Date)*

PART A. Using the answer line, complete each item below with the correct word from the box.

a. **amazed**	c. **effort**
b. **confident**	d. **uncertain**

_____ 1. I was up late last night, so it was a real . . ? . . to get up early this morning.

_____ 2. I hope the soup I made tastes all right. I was . . ? . . how much salt to put in it.

_____ 3. People were . . ? . . when a woman in Iowa gave birth to seven healthy babies.

_____ 4. Paul never tells lies, so I am . . ? . . that what he told me is the truth.

PART B. Using the answer line, complete each item below with the correct word from the box.

e. **donate**	g. **purpose**
f. **locate**	h. **sincere**

_____ 5. Making dinner in my sister's kitchen was hard, because I didn't know where to . . ? . . anything.

_____ 6. Gordon was . . ? . . about starting to exercise more. In the last week, he has gone for a run or a bike ride every day.

_____ 7. Jeri went downtown for the . . ? . . of applying for a job.

_____ 8. Around the holidays, bell-ringers for the Salvation Army encourage people to . . ? . . their spare change to help others.

SCORE: (Number correct) _____ × 12.5 = _____ %

Name: _____

Mastery Test: *Chapter 14 (Malls; As Good As It Looks?)*

PART A. Using the answer line, complete each item below with the correct word from the box.

a. **dismissed**	c. **opinion**
b. **guarantee**	d. **resolved**

_____ 1. The mayor . . ? . . the reporters when they began asking questions she did not want to answer.

_____ 2. Rita has . . ? . . to visit her grandmother in the nursing home at least once a week.

_____ 3. The store has this simple . . ? . . on every item it sells: "If you're not happy with this product, we'll give you your money back."

_____ 4. In my . . ? . ., you look best in dark green clothing and worst in light pink.

PART B. Using the answer line, complete each item below with the correct word from the box.

e. **disgusts**	g. **inspect**
f. **ideal**	h. **prevent**

_____ 5. The proper use of a seat belt can . . ? . . injury in many car crashes.

_____ 6. Cleaning up his puppy's "accidents" . . ? . . Dave, but he knows it is part of being a pet owner.

_____ 7. The water in the swimming pool is . . ? . . —warm enough to be comfortable, but cool enough to be refreshing.

_____ 8. Before putting their children in a day-care center, parents should . . ? . . the center carefully.

SCORE: (Number correct) _____ × 12.5 = _____ %

Name: _____

Mastery Test: *Chapter 15 (A Belief in Flying; She Tries)*

PART A. Using the answer line, complete each item below with the correct word from the box.

a. **advice**	c. **impossible**
b. **defeat**	d. **permit**

_____ 1. When you have a decision to make, whom do you ask for . . ? . .?

_____ 2. I can't go to work. It is . . ? . . to travel on these icy roads.

_____ 3. No one can . . ? . . our school's top swimmer—she's the best.

_____ 4. Will you . . ? . . me to borrow your car tomorrow?

PART B. Using the answer line, complete each item below with the correct word from the box.

e. **cautious**	g. **necessary**
f. **defect**	h. **provided**

_____ 5. It is . . ? . . to file an income-tax return by April 15 of each year.

_____ 6. This video must have a . . ? . .—the picture is fuzzy and difficult to watch.

_____ 7. During the long race, people standing by the roadside . . ? . . drinks of water for the runners as they passed.

_____ 8. People who roller-blade should be . . ? . . and wear a helmet and knee pads.

SCORE: (Number correct) _____ × 12.5 = _____ %

Name: _____

Mastery Test: *Chapter 16 (Play Now, Pay Later; Many Faces)*

PART A. Using the answer line, complete each item below with the correct word from the box.

a. **arranged**	c. **hollow**
b. **continue**	d. **supposed**

_____ 1. If you blow into something . . ? . . , like an empty soda bottle, you can make a musical sound.

_____ 2. I . . ? . . the store would be closed today, since it's a holiday, but in fact it was open.

_____ 3. Luisa . . ? . . her office so everything she needed was within an arm's reach.

_____ 4. If you . . ? . . teasing the cat, you are likely to get scratched.

PART B. Using the answer line, complete each item below with the correct word from the box.

e. **expert**	g. **personal**
f. **panic**	h. **regrets**

_____ 5. Cinda woke up from her frightening dream with a feeling of . . ? . . .

_____ 6. Tomas is an . . ? . . at playing guitar, so many people ask him for lessons.

_____ 7. On a first date, people usually don't talk about very . . ? . . subjects. They have those conversations when they know each other better.

_____ 8. Olivia . . ? . . getting a large tattoo on her arm, but there's nothing she can do about it now.

SCORE: (Number correct) _____ × 12.5 = _____ %

Mastery Test: *Chapter 17 (Soaps; Keeping the Customer Happy)*

PART A. Using the answer line, complete each item below with the correct word from the box.

a. **admits**	c. **encourage**
b. **dull**	d. **intimate**

_____ 1. To . . ? . . her son to read more, Lila began taking him to the library every week.

_____ 2. "Nothing to do, no one to talk to, nowhere to go," complained Eric. "This is a really . . ? . . day!"

_____ 3. Although Stan never smokes at home anymore, he . . ? . . that he sometimes has a cigarette when he's out with his friends.

_____ 4. Kindergarten teachers often hear the most . . ? . . details of family life from their little students, who don't realize that some topics are private.

PART B. Using the answer line, complete each item below with the correct word from the box.

e. **available**	g. **experiment**
f. **contributes**	h. **portions**

_____ 5. Computer magazines are . . ? . . nearly everywhere these days. You can find them in drugstores, bookstores, and grocery stores.

_____ 6. A healthy diet is not only a matter of what you eat, but how large the . . ? . . are.

_____ 7. At work, we have "brainstorming sessions," where everyone . . ? . . his or her ideas as quickly as possible.

_____ 8. Shelley likes to . . ? . . with her hair. Sometimes it's up, sometimes it's down, and sometimes it's all the colors of the rainbow.

SCORE: (Number correct) _____ × 12.5 = _____ %

Mastery Test: *Chapter 18 (Fake "Cure"; The Jobs Everyone Hates)*

PART A. Using the answer line, complete each item below with the correct word from the box.

a. **contains**	c. **effective**
b. **depend**	d. **involved**

_____ 1. Mom makes a casserole that . . ? . . tuna, noodles, mushrooms, and sour cream.

_____ 2. Students in the fourth, fifth, and sixth grades were . . ? . . in planning the new school playground.

_____ 3. Since there are no buses where he lives, Geraldo has to . . ? . . on his car to get him to work.

_____ 4. For me, making a "Things To Do" list is an . . ? . . way of getting done things I might otherwise forget.

PART B. Using the answer line, complete each item below with the correct word from the box.

e. **compete**	g. **gradual**
f. **envy**	h. **intense**

_____ 5. In the last few years, there has been a . . ? . . change in my father's hair color. It has slowly turned from brown to gray.

_____ 6. When her baby brother was born, Shannon felt . . ? . . jealousy over all the attention he received.

_____ 7. The world's best athletes . . ? . . in the Olympics.

_____ 8. The kids who walk to school . . ? . . the ones who get to ride the bus, but the bus-riders wish that they could walk.

SCORE: (Number correct) _____ × 12.5 = _____ %

Name: _____

Mastery Test: *Chapter 19 (A Young Librarian; No More Harm)*

PART A. Using the answer line, complete each item below with the correct word from the box.

a. **collapse**	c. **modest**
b. **grief**	d. **similar**

_____ 1. People would like Peter better if he were more . . ? . . . He's always bragging about how wonderful he is.

_____ 2. Reading the news stories about the Oklahoma City bombing, Lisa was filled with . . ? . . for those who had died and their families.

_____ 3. The real diamond and the fake one are so . . ? . . that only a jeweler can tell them apart.

_____ 4. Nikki set up a long line of dominoes, then knocked over the first one and watched the rest . . ? . . .

PART B. Using the answer line, complete each item below with the correct word from the box.

e. **alarmed**	g. **relieved**
f. **defend**	h. **victims**

_____ 5. Mrs. Hendrix was worried about her health, but the doctor told her good news that . . ? . . her.

_____ 6. Our dog is always friendly with visitors, but he would . . ? . . us against anyone who tried to hurt us.

_____ 7. The Patels are thinking about closing their store, because they have been the . . ? . . of three robberies in the last year.

_____ 8. The news that there was a house fire in her neighborhood . . ? . . Cara.

SCORE: (Number correct) _____ × 12.5 = _____ %

Name: _____

Mastery Test: *Chapter 20 (Man or Machine; Struck by Lightning)*

PART A. Using the answer line, complete each item below with the correct word from the box.

a. **confusion**	c. **emerged**
b. **distant**	d. **refuses**

_____ 1. Mike and Brenda were late for the movie, because there was some . . ? . . about where they were supposed to meet. She went to his house, and he went to hers.

_____ 2. My little sister . . ? . . to eat vegetables, so Mom sneaks them into things like meatloaf and spaghetti sauce.

_____ 3. The faint sound of . . ? . . thunder warned us that a storm was on its way.

_____ 4. I stood a long time in the empty store before a clerk . . ? . . from the storage room and said, "Can I help you?"

PART B. Using the answer line, complete each item below with the correct word from the box.

e. **decrease**	g. **realized**
f. **incident**	h. **survived**

_____ 5. My parents took me to an eye doctor when they . . ? . . I needed glasses.

_____ 6. The newspaper reported on an . . ? . . in which two gangs of teenagers got into a fight.

_____ 7. A cat who was accidentally shut into a box somehow . . ? . . for three weeks, and lived to a healthy old age.

_____ 8. Washing your hands often can . . ? . . your chance of catching a cold.

SCORE: (Number correct) _____ × 12.5 = _____ %

Name: _____

Mastery Test: *Chapter 21 (Whose Fault?; Forests Full of Life)*

PART A. Using the answer line, complete each item below with the correct word from the box.

a. **persuade**	c. **reveal**
b. **quarrel**	d. **stubborn**

_____ 1. George will not dance, and nothing his girlfriend says can . . ? . . him to change his mind.

_____ 2. Don't . . ? . . the end of the movie to me—I want to be surprised when I see it.

_____ 3. The day after their . . ? . ., both Alysha and Suzette felt ashamed, so they apologized to one another.

_____ 4. The . . ? . . child kept saying she wanted the purple and green shoes, and that she would not wear any other pair.

PART B. Using the answer line, complete each item below with the correct word from the box.

e. **excess**	g. **separated**
f. **reaction**	h. **tremendous**

_____ 5. Irene used most of the icing to decorate the cake, then gave the . . ? . . icing to her children so they could eat it.

_____ 6. The flood did . . ? . . damage to the city. Hundreds of homes were destroyed, thousands of people were homeless, and millions of dollars were lost.

_____ 7. When her family jumped out and shouted "Surprise!" little Emily's . . ? . . was to burst into tears.

_____ 8. Jeanine went through all her clothes and . . ? . . them into two piles—those she wears often, and those she hardly ever wears. Then she gave the second pile away.

SCORE: (Number correct) _____ × 12.5 = _____ %

Mastery Test: *Chapter 22 (Animal in Danger; Simple Life)*

PART A. Using the answer line, complete each item below with the correct word from the box.

a. **disaster**	c. **scarce**
b. **fascinates**	d. **tolerate**

_____ 1. The play was a . . ? . . . The lead actor forgot his lines, the scenery fell down, and most of the audience walked out before the end.

_____ 2. The idea of life on other planets . . ? . . many people. They find it interesting to think what other life forms might be like.

_____ 3. Quiet moments are . . ? . . in our house—there's almost always some noise or conversation going on.

_____ 4. My grandparents won't . . ? . . bad manners. They are quick to correct a grandchild who they think is being rude

PART B. Using the answer line, complete each item below with the correct word from the box.

e. **generous**	g. **predict**
f. **increase**	h. **progress**

_____ 5. The workers were happy to hear that their pay would . . ? . . in the coming year.

_____ 6. Ginny is known for being . . ? . . . When new neighbors move in on her street, she always buys them a little present.

_____ 7. With the leaders of the two countries so angry at one another, many experts . . ? . . there will soon be war.

_____ 8. Although she has lived in this country for only six months, Mei Lin has made wonderful . . ? . . in learning English.

SCORE: (Number correct) _____ × 12.5 = _____ %

Name: _____

Mastery Test: *Chapter 23 (Taking a Break; Working and Living)*

PART A. Using the answer line, complete each item below with the correct word from the box.

a. **humor**	c. **selected**
b. **notice**	d. **weary**

_____ 1. To be a good driver, it's not enough to pay attention to what you are doing. You have to . . ? . . what the other drivers are doing, too.

_____ 2. As she shopped for her dinner party, Lily . . ? . . the most perfect fruits, vegetables, and fish she could find.

_____ 3. "If you wait until the last minute to write your report, you know what will happen," warned the teacher. "You will stay up late and be too . . ? . . to do a good job."

_____ 4. Maddie uses . . ? . . to try to get out of trouble. If her mother is angry with her, Maddie quickly tells a joke.

PART B. Using the answer line, complete each item below with the correct word from the box.

e. **detail**	g. **occupy**
f. **glared**	h. **performed**

_____ 5. My boss pays attention to every little . . ? . . of his clothing. For instance, the handkerchief in his pocket always matches his tie.

_____ 6. I didn't realize Hernando was angry with me until I noticed how he . . ? . . at me when I walked past.

_____ 7. After practicing for weeks, the second-graders . . ? . . their favorite songs for the older students.

_____ 8. Three hermit crabs . . ? . . the small wire cage on the window sill.

SCORE: (Number correct) _____ × 12.5 = _____ %

Mastery Test: *Chapter 24 (The Horror of Hate; Time for Thanks)*

PART A. Using the answer line, complete each item below with the correct word from the box.

a. **condemned**	c. **isolated**
b. **imagine**	d. **unite**

_____ 1. After his wife's death, Mr. Jackson . . ? . . himself, refusing to see even his close friends.

_____ 2. "Listen to this music," said the art teacher, "and draw what you . . ? . . the sound would look like if you could see it."

_____ 3. The entire city . . ? . . the cruel man who robbed the little girls' lemonade stand.

_____ 4. Motorcycle lovers from all over the country will . . ? . . next weekend at a giant motorcycle fair in this town.

PART B. Using the answer line, complete each item below with the correct word from the box.

e. **embraces**	g. **familiar**
f. **expressed**	h. **support**

_____ 5. The angry look on Mark's face . . ? . . his feelings as well as words could have.

_____ 6. "The average human needs at least eight hugs a day," claims Judy, explaining why she . . ? . . her friends whenever they meet.

_____ 7. Bugs Bunny and Mickey Mouse are two cartoon characters that are . . ? . . to children in almost every part of the world.

_____ 8. I don't often shop in big department stores. I prefer to . . ? . . local merchants who run their own small shops.

SCORE: (Number correct) _____ × 12.5 = _____ %

Name: _____

Mastery Test: *Chapter 25 (A Surprising Change; Just for Fun)*

PART A. Using the answer line, complete each item below with the correct word from the box.

a. **bold**	c. **pretended**
b. **develop**	d. **solution**

_____ 1. Most of the children were too shy to speak to their new classmate, but one
. . ? . . little girl marched up and said, "Hi! What's your name?"

_____ 2. Roger foolishly . . ? . . to be rich in order to impress his new girlfriend.

_____ 3. It is surprising how a little fish-like tadpole can . . ? . . into a frog.

_____ 4. Here's a riddle: What's black and white and black and white and black and
white? And here's the . . ? . . : a penguin rolling down a hill.

PART B. Using the answer line, complete each item below with the correct word from the box.

e. **admire**	g. **expect**
f. **comments**	h. **insists**

_____ 5. Rita's . . ? . . about the new restaurant did not make me want to go there.
She said the food was bad, the prices were high, and the service was slow.

_____ 6. I . . ? . . my aunt for returning to school at age 40 and earning her high-
school degree—that took a lot of courage and hard work.

_____ 7. Because his friends . . ? . . Keith to be late (he always is), they usually tell
him to arrive someplace fifteen minutes before they really need him.

_____ 8. Don . . ? . . that he is six feet tall, but he doesn't look that tall to me.

SCORE: (Number correct) _____ × 12.5 = _____ %

Name: _____

Mastery Test: *Chapter 26 (Little Lies; Rudeness at the Movies)*

PART A. Using the answer line, complete each item below with the correct word from the box.

a. **appeared**	c. **conceal**
b. **common**	d. **mentioned**

_____ 1. The couple at the next table . . ? . . to be fighting, although I could not hear what they were saying.

_____ 2. After she walked into a door and hurt herself, Selma wore makeup to . . ? . . her black eye.

_____ 3. At our school, blue jeans and T-shirts are the most . . ? . . outfit. Almost everyone wears them.

_____ 4. I didn't know that Mrs. Hamilton had been born in another country until she . . ? . . growing up in England.

PART B. Using the answer line, complete each item below with the correct word from the box.

e. **attracts**	g. **irritate**
f. **enormous**	h. **surrounded**

_____ 5. A burning house always . . ? . . a crowd of curious people.

_____ 6. On a long car trip, children often . . ? . . their parents by asking over and over, "Are we there yet?"

_____ 7. We stared at the . . ? . . palace, wondering what it would be like to live in such a huge place.

_____ 8. As she set up things her new apartment, Liza . . ? . . herself with pictures of family and friends so that she would feel at home.

SCORE: (Number correct) _____ × 12.5 = _____ %

Name: _____

Mastery Test: *Chapter 27 (Drinking; A Life Out of Balance)*

PART A. Using the answer line, complete each item below with the correct word from the box.

a. **achieve**	c. **injury**
b. **condition**	d. **major**

_____ 1. In seven more months, Greg will . . ? . . his dream of becoming a college graduate.

_____ 2. Luisa has to sleep on her living-room couch until her leg . . ? . . heals. She can't climb the stairs.

_____ 3. Before they try to sell their house, the Martins will do some painting and repairs so that it is in good . . ? . . .

_____ 4. "Is there a little problem?" Marie asked the police officer who stopped her. "No, ma'am," he answered. "There is a . . ? . . problem."

PART B. Using the answer line, complete each item below with the correct word from the box.

e. **duty**	g. **seldom**
f. **exhaust**	h. **value**

_____ 5. The puppies play until they . . ? . . themselves, then sleep for hours.

_____ 6. Gold and jewels and money are nice, but nothing is of greater . . ? . . than a good education.

_____ 7. It is Ali's weekly . . ? . . to mow the lawn.

_____ 8. Because she doesn't see well at night, Aunt Lucy . . ? . . goes out in the evening.

SCORE: (Number correct) _____ × 12.5 = _____ %

Name: _____

Mastery Test: *Chapter 28 (Animals Were First; Call Waiting)*

PART A. Using the answer line, complete each item below with the correct word from the box.

a. **advanced**	c. **grasped**
b. **delicate**	d. **succeed**

_____ 1. Famous old papers, like the Declaration of Independence, are kept in special glass boxes. They are so . . ? . . that they would fall apart if they were handled.

_____ 2. As we said goodbye, my friend . . ? . . my hand tightly and said, "I'll miss you."

_____ 3. The old saying, "If at first you don't . . ? . ., try, try again," means that you have to work hard in order to do well.

_____ 4. Moving slowly and carefully, the cat . . ? . . toward the mouse.

PART B. Using the answer line, complete each item below with the correct word from the box.

e. **considered**	g. **praise**
f. **interrupted**	h. **request**

_____ 5. Ms. Lopez always finds something to . . ? . . in her students' work, as well as things to correct.

_____ 6. Roger . . ? . . joining the Army, but decided to attend college instead.

_____ 7. An emergency weather report . . ? . . my favorite TV program.

_____ 8. "I have one . . ? . .," said the magician to the audience. "Please do not take photographs during the show."

SCORE: (Number correct) _____ × 12.5 = _____ %

Name: _____

Mastery Test: *Chapter 29 (Cab Driver; Thoughts at the Mall)*

PART A. Using the answer line, complete each item below with the correct word from the box.

a. **attempted**	c. **permanent**
b. **courteous**	d. **recognize**

_____ 1. Taylor . . ? . . to apologize to Sandra after their fight, but she would not listen to him.

_____ 2. Little children may not realize that death is . . ? . . . For instance, a child may ask, "Is Grandma going to be alive again next week?"

_____ 3. The . . ? . . thing to do when you are given a present you don't like is to say, "Thank you very much. It was so kind of you to think of me."

_____ 4. When we drove by our old house, we could hardly . . ? . . it. The new owners had built an addition and painted it a new color.

PART B. Using the answer line, complete each item below with the correct word from the box.

e. **explore**	g. **imitate**
f. **hopeless**	h. **sufficient**

_____ 5. Often on a Saturday, Marv and Janet will drive to a little town and . . ? . . it just for fun.

_____ 6. Parrots are clever birds that can . . ? . . human speech.

_____ 7. I felt sorry for my brother after he lost his job and his girlfriend in one week. I could tell he felt quite . . ? . . .

_____ 8. If there is . . ? . . time after dinner, I'd like to go visit our new neighbors.

> *SCORE:* (Number correct) _____ × 12.5 = _____ %

Name: _____

Mastery Test: *Chapter 30 (Birth of Red Cross; To Spank or Not)*

PART A. Using the answer line, complete each item below with the correct word from the box.

a. **assists**	c. **examined**
b. **enemy**	d. **positive**

_____ 1. Every night after dinner, Raoul . . ? . . his sons with their homework.

_____ 2. The doctor . . ? . . Lois after the accident and told her that she was just shaken up, but not really hurt.

_____ 3. I don't know why Jim thinks Hank is his . . ? . . . I don't think even Jim knows—he's hated Hank for so long that it's just become a habit.

_____ 4. Lori is such a . . ? . . person that she even found something good in breaking her leg. "I really needed to catch up on my reading anyway, and now I'll have a chance!" she said.

PART B. Using the answer line, complete each item below with the correct word from the box.

e. **competent**	g. **samples**
f. **flaw**	h. **urge**

_____ 5. Gary is a . . ? . . student who almost always earns A's and B's.

_____ 6. If you can't decide which flavor of ice cream to order, the clerk will give you tiny . . ? . . of several to taste.

_____ 7. I couldn't figure out what I did wrong in the math problem until I studied it carefully. Then I saw the . . ? . . in my addition.

_____ 8. Jake woke up at 3 a.m. with the . . ? . . to get up and make a tunafish and onion sandwich.

SCORE: (Number correct) _____ × 12.5 = _____ %

Chapter 1 (The Nose Knows; Barbie)

1. b. fact
2. d. suggest
3. c. odor
4. a. curious
5. g. flexible
6. f. cancel
7. e. agreement
8. h. prepare

Chapter 2 (Feeling Blue; A Late Love Letter)

1. c. produced
2. a. entertains
3. d. tension
4. b. experience
5. g. negative
6. e. daily
7. f. identify
8. h. original

Chapter 3 (Ads That Lie; Horrible Hiccups)

1. c. protect
2. b. event
3. a. conclusion
4. d. talent
5. f. humble
6. e. attack
7. g. minor
8. h. volunteer

Chapter 4 (An Upsetting Dream; A King's Mistake)

1. c. inspired
2. d. unusual
3. b. embarrassed
4. a. claims
5. g. precious
6. e. accused
7. h. public
8. f. pleasant

Chapter 5 (Be Proud of Age; Making Anger Work)

1. c. emphasized
2. a. benefited
3. d. logical
4. b. delayed
5. g. tempt
6. e. rivals
7. f. satisfy
8. h. vacant

Chapter 6 (Customers; Stuck in the Middle)

1. b. motivated
2. d. suspect
3. a. definite
4. c. specific
5. e. fortunate
6. g. oppose
7. h. refers
8. f. leisure

Chapter 7 (Joy of Ice Cream; A Noisy Apartment)

1. d. popular
2. a. devour
3. c. occasions
4. b. modern
5. h. distressed
6. e. aware
7. f. constant
8. g. discovered

Chapter 8 (Nuts in the Senate; Calling Dr. Leech)

1. c. glanced
2. d. introduce
3. b. failure
4. a. created
5. e. ability
6. h. labor
7. f. damage
8. g. gratitude

Chapter 9 (TV and Violence; Ready for a Pet?)

1. b. excuse
2. a. avoid
3. d. normal
4. c. includes
5. e. helpless
6. h. struggle
7. f. intended
8. g. sociable

Chapter 10 (Help for Shy People; Laughing Matter)

1. d. timid
2. b. numerous
3. a. damp
4. c. requires
5. f. ignore
6. e. approached
7. h. previous
8. g. loyal

Chapter 11 (Taking Risks; Bad Manners Hurt)

1. c. opportunity
2. a. capable
3. d. resist
4. b. observes
5. e. careless
6. g. reversed
7. h. tradition
8. f. furious

Chapter 12 (Two Different Sisters; Honest Abe)

1. b. distract
2. a. comfortable
3. d. sensitive
4. c. insulting
5. e. allow
6. g. respect
7. h. wonder
8. f. persisted

Chapter 13 (Ready to Do Well; Advertising for Date)

1. c. effort
2. d. uncertain
3. a. amazed
4. b. confident
5. f. locate
6. h. sincere
7. g. purpose
8. e. donate

Chapter 14 (Malls; As Good As It Looks?)

1. a. dismissed
2. d. resolved
3. b. guarantee
4. c. opinion
5. h. prevent
6. e. disgusts
7. f. ideal
8. g. inspect

Chapter 15 (A Belief in Flying; She Tries)

1. a. advice
2. c. impossible
3. b. defeat
4. d. permit
5. g. necessary
6. f. defect
7. h. provided
8. e. cautious

Chapter 16 (Play Now, Pay Later; Many Faces)

1. c. hollow
2. d. supposed
3. a. arranged
4. b. continue
5. f. panic
6. e. expert
7. g. personal
8. h. regrets

Chapter 17 (Soaps: Keeping the Customer Happy)
1. c. encourage
2. b. dull
3. a. admits
4. d. intimate
5. e. available
6. h. portions
7. f. contributes
8. g. experiment

Chapter 18 (Fake "Cure": The Jobs Everyone Hates)
1. a. contains
2. d. involved
3. b. depend
4. c. effective
5. g. gradual
6. h. intense
7. e. compete
8. f. envy

Chapter 19 (A Young Librarian; No More Harm)
1. c. modest
2. b. grief
3. d. similar
4. a. collapse
5. g. relieved
6. f. defend
7. h. victims
8. e. alarmed

Chapter 20 (Man or Machine; Struck by Lightning)
1. a. confusion
2. d. refuses
3. b. distant
4. c. emerged
5. g. realized
6. f. incident
7. h. survived
8. e. decrease

Chapter 21 (Whose Fault?; Forests Full of Life)
1. a. persuade
2. c. reveal
3. b. quarrel
4. d. stubborn
5. e. excess
6. h. tremendous
7. f. reaction
8. g. separated

Chapter 22 (Animal in Danger; Simple Life)
1. a. disaster
2. b. fascinates
3. c. scarce
4. d. tolerate
5. f. increase
6. e. generous
7. g. predict
8. h. progress

Chapter 23 (Taking a Break; Working and Living)
1. b. notice
2. c. selected
3. d. weary
4. a. humor
5. e. detail
6. f. glared
7. h. performed
8. g. occupy

Chapter 24 (The Horror of Hate; Time for Thanks)
1. c. isolated
2. b. imagine
3. a. condemned
4. d. unite
5. f. expressed
6. e. embraces
7. g. familiar
8. h. support

Chapter 25 (A Surprising Change; Just for Fun)
1. a. bold
2. c. pretended
3. b. develop
4. d. solution
5. f. comments
6. e. admire
7. g. expect
8. h. insists

Chapter 26 (Little Lies; Rudeness at the Movies)
1. a. appeared
2. c. conceal
3. b. common
4. d. mentioned
5. e. attracts
6. g. irritate
7. f. enormous
8. h. surrounded

Chapter 27 (Drinking; A Life Out of Balance)
1. a. achieve
2. c. injury
3. b. condition
4. d. major
5. f. exhaust
6. h. value
7. e. duty
8. g. seldom

Chapter 28 (Animals Were First; Call Waiting)
1. b. delicate
2. c. grasped
3. d. succeed
4. a. advanced
5. g. praise
6. e. considered
7. f. interrupted
8. h. request

Chapter 29 (Cab Driver; Thoughts at the Mall)
1. a. attempted
2. c. permanent
3. b. courteous
4. d. recognize
5. e. explore
6. g. imitate
7. f. hopeless
8. h. sufficient

Chapter 30 (Birth of Red Cross; To Spank or Not)
1. a. assists
2. c. examined
3. b. enemy
4. d. positive
5. e. competent
6. g. samples
7. f. flaw
8. h. urge

Answers to the Chapter Activities in
GROUNDWORK FOR A BETTER VOCABULARY

Chapter 1 (Johnny Appleseed; The Lovable Leech?)

Ten Words in Context		Matching Words with Definitions		Check 1		Check 2		Related Words		Word Work		Word Parts/Syn-Ant/Analogies		Final Check	
1. c	6. c	1. 3	6. 1	1. j	6. g	1–2. e, g		1. d	6. h	1. c	6. a	1. c	6. g	1. b	6. g
2. a	7. c	2. 6	7. 7	2. c	7. f	3–4. j, f		2. a	7. j	2. b	7. b	2. b	7. i	2. d	7. i
3. c	8. a	3. 2	8. 10	3. e	8. a	5–6. h, b		3. b	8. f	3. c	8. c	3. d	8. j	3. a	8. f
4. b	9. b	4. 9	9. 8	4. i	9. h	7–8. c, a		4. c	9. g	4. a	9. a	4. e	9. h	4. c	9. h
5. a	10. c	5. 4	10. 5	5. d	10. b	9–10. d. i		5. e	10. i	5. a	10. c	5. a	10. f	5. e	10. j

Chapter 2 (Finding Fault—And What to Do About It; What Do Your Hobbies Reveal About You?)

Ten Words in Context		Matching Words with Definitions		Check 1		Check 2		Related Words		Word Work		Word Parts/Syn-Ant/Analogies		Final Check	
1. b	6. c	1. 9	6. 4	1. i	6. h	1–2. d, c		1. e	6. i	1. c	6. b	1. b	6. d	1. c	6. g
2. c	7. a	2. 2	7. 5	2. f	7. c	3–4. b, e		2. c	7. f	2. a	7. a	2. b	7. a	2. d	7. h
3. c	8. c	3. 3	8. 8	3. g	8. a	5–6. f, h		3. d	8. g	3. c	8. b	3. a	8. b	3. e	8. i
4. c	9. b	4. 7	9. 1	4. j	9. e	7–8. i, g		4. a	9. j	4. a	9. c	4. d	9. b	4. b	9. f
5. a	10. b	5. 6	10. 10	5. b	10. d	9–10. a, j		5. b	10. h	5. b	10. b	5. c	10. c	5. a	10. j

Chapter 3 (Fixing Up Furniture; Barbara's Date with Her Cousin)

Ten Words in Context		Matching Words with Definitions		Check 1		Check 2		Related Words		Word Work		Word Parts/Syn-Ant/Analogies		Final Check	
1. c	6. a	1. 5	6. 9	1. b	6. h	1–2. e, f		1. c	6. g	1. c	6. a	1. b	6. j	1. b	6. g
2. b	7. b	2. 3	7. 6	2. e	7. f	3–4. j, g		2. a	7. j	2. a	7. c	2. e	7. i	2. e	7. j
3. c	8. b	3. 4	8. 8	3. a	8. c	5–6. b, c		3. d	8. f	3. b	8. b	3. d	8. f	3. a	8. h
4. a	9. a	4. 2	9. 7	4. j	9. g	7–8. i, d		4. e	9. i	4. c	9. c	4. c	9. g	4. c	9. i
5. b	10. c	5. 10	10. 1	5. d	10. i	9–10. a, h		5. b	10. h	5. b	10. a	5. a	10. h	5. d	10. f

Chapter 4 (The Vacuum-Cleaner Salesman; Peace at Last)

Ten Words in Context		Matching Words with Definitions		Check 1		Check 2		Related Words		Word Work		Word Parts/Syn-Ant/Analogies		Final Check	
1. b	6. a	1. 8	6. 9	1. j	6. c	1–2. e, i		1. b	6. i	1. b	6. c	1. d	6. a	1. b	6. g
2. a	7. b	2. 1	7. 5	2. b	7. d	3–4. j, c		2. d	7. g	2. c	7. b	2. b	7. d	2. d	7. i
3. a	8. b	3. 3	8. 2	3. g	8. f	5–6. a, g		3. c	8. j	3. c	8. c	3. a	8. c	3. a	8. h
4. c	9. b	4. 7	9. 10	4. a	9. h	7–8. d, f		4. a	9. h	4. a	9. a	4. a	9. b	4. e	9. f
5. b	10. c	5. 6	10. 4	5. i	10. e	9–10. h, b		5. e	10. f	5. b	10. b	5. c	10. b	5. c	10. j

Chapter 5 (Study Skills to the Rescue!; How to Control Children)

Ten Words in Context		Matching Words with Definitions		Check 1		Check 2		Related Words		Word Work		Word Parts/Syn-Ant/Analogies		Final Check	
1. b	6. b	1. 8	6. 5	1. i	6. f	1–2. a, b		1. e	6. i	1. c	6. c	1. a	6. b	1. b	6. g
2. c	7. b	2. 2	7. 3	2. j	7. c	3–4. i, g		2. d	7. h	2. a	7. b	2. c	7. a	2. a	7. i
3. a	8. c	3. 9	8. 4	3. a	8. g	5–6. d, h		3. a	8. f	3. c	8. c	3. d	8. d	3. e	8. h
4. c	9. a	4. 6	9. 7	4. d	9. e	7–8. j, e		4. c	9. j	4. b	9. c	4. c	9. d	4. c	9. f
5. c	10. c	5. 1	10. 10	5. h	10. b	9–10. c, f		5. b	10. g	5. c	10. a	5. d	10. a	5. d	10. j

Chapter 6 (Toasters; A Mean Man)

Ten Words in Context		Matching Words with Definitions		Check 1		Check 2		Related Words		Word Work		Word Parts/Syn-Ant/Analogies		Final Check	
1. b	6. c	1. 7	6. 2	1. j	6. b	1–2. i, c		1. d	6. h	1. d	6. b	1. d	6. h	1. d	6. i
2. a	7. c	2. 4	7. 8	2. a	7. c	3–4. f, j		2. a	7. g	2. e	7. c	2. c	7. g	2. e	7. g
3. a	8. b	3. 3	8. 9	3. f	8. d	5–6. g, e		3. b	8. i	3. a	8. a	3. b	8. j	3. b	8. h
4. b	9. c	4. 6	9. 1	4. i	9. g	7–8. b, a		4. c	9. j	4. b	9. c	4. e	9. f	4. a	9. f
5. a	10. b	5. 5	10. 10	5. h	10. e	9–10. h, d		5. e	10. f	5. c	10. b	5. a	10. i	5. c	10. j

Chapter 7 (A Special Memory; Watch Your Manners!)

Ten Words in Context		Matching Words with Definitions		Check 1		Check 2		Related Words		Word Work		Word Parts/Syn-Ant/Analogies		Final Check	
1. c	6. c	1. 9	6. 8	1. g	6. a	1–2. a, b		1. e	6. j	1. b	6. b	1. c	6. a	1. b	6. g
2. c	7. c	2. 7	7. 3	2. c	7. f	3–4. e, g		2. a	7. h	2. a	7. c	2. d	7. b	2. d	7. h
3. b	8. c	3. 6	8. 10	3. j	8. d	5–6. j, i		3. b	8. i	3. c	8. b	3. d	8. d	3. c	8. f
4. a	9. c	4. 4	9. 2	4. b	9. i	7–8. c, d		4. d	9. f	4. a	9. b	4. a	9. c	4. a	9. j
5. a	10. b	5. 5	10. 1	5. h	10. e	9–10. f, h		5. c	10. g	5. c	10. a	5. b	10. a	5. e	10. i

Chapter 8 (Big Brothers and Sisters; Kevin's First Date)

Ten Words in Context	Matching Words with Definitions	Check 1	Check 2	Related Words	Word Work	Word Parts/Syn-Ant/Analogies	Final Check
1. a 6. c	1. 5 6. 1	1. f 6. a	1–2. e, j	1. b 6. h	1. c 6. a	1. c 6. g	1. a 6. f
2. c 7. a	2. 2 7. 4	2. h 7. e	3–4. i, a	2. d 7. f	2. d 7. b	2. d 7. j	2. b 7. i
3. b 8. c	3. 9 8. 8	3. i 8. d	5–6. b, f	3. c 8. i	3. e 8. c	3. b 8. f	3. e 8. h
4. b 9. a	4. 10 9. 3	4. b 9. g	7–8. h, g	4. a 9. g	4. b 9. a	4. a 9. h	4. d 9. g
5. c 10. c	5. 7 10. 6	5. j 10. c	9–10. d, c	5. e 10. j	5. d 10. b	5. e 10. i	5. c 10. j

Chapter 9 (Differences in a Gym Program; Teaching A Lesson)

Ten Words in Context	Matching Words with Definitions	Check 1	Check 2	Related Words	Word Work	Word Parts/Syn-Ant/Analogies	Final Check
1. c 6. a	1. 10 6. 4	1. b 6. g	1–2. j, e	1. b 6. d	1. c 6. c	1. d 6. b	1. a 6. g
2. a 7. c	2. 7 7. 5	2. i 7. c	3–4. b, h	2. a 7. b	2. b 7. b	2. c 7. c	2. e 7. h
3. b 8. c	3. 2 8. 3	3. h 8. e	5–6. i, c	3. d 8. a	3. b 8. c	3. d 8. d	3. b 8. f
4. c 9. a	4. 8 9. 6	4. j 9. d	7–8. d, f	4. c 9. c	4. c 9. c	4. a 9. a	4. c 9. j
5. c 10. a	5. 1 10. 9	5. f 10. a	9–10. g, a	5. e 10. e	5. a 10. a	5. a 10. b	5. d 10. i

Chapter 10 (Knowing How to Argue; A Change of School, A Change of Heart)

Ten Words in Context	Matching Words with Definitions	Check 1	Check 2	Related Words	Word Work	Word Parts/Syn-Ant/Analogies	Final Check
1. c 6. c	1. 1 6. 2	1. c 6. i	1–2. a, e	1. d 6. j	1. b 6. b	1. a 6. b	1. b 6. g
2. c 7. b	2. 7 7. 5	2. b 7. d	3–4. b, c	2. b 7. h	2. c 7. b	2. c 7. d	2. d 7. i
3. b 8. b	3. 9 8. 10	3. f 8. a	5–6. i, j	3. c 8. i	3. a 8. b	3. c 8. b	3. a 8. f
4. a 9. c	4. 3 9. 6	4. g 9. e	7–8. d, f	4. a 9. f	4. c 9. c	4. a 9. a	4. e 9. h
5. c 10. a	5. 4 10. 8	5. j 10. h	9–10. g, h	5. e 10. g	5. b 10. a	5. b 10. b	5. c 10. j

Chapter 11 (Coming Out of a Coma; The Office Doughnut Contest)

Ten Words in Context	Matching Words with Definitions	Check 1	Check 2	Related Words	Word Work	Word Parts/Syn-Ant/Analogies	Final Check
1. c 6. a	1. 10 6. 8	1. f 6. b	1–2. i, c	1. d 6. f	1. b 6. c	1. d 6. h	1. a 6. f
2. b 7. a	2. 5 7. 1	2. d 7. h	3–4. d, f	2. a 7. j	2. e 7. c	2. c 7. g	2. c 7. h
3. c 8. b	3. 2 8. 3	3. g 8. i	5–6. e, j	3. b 8. g	3. c 8. b	3. a 8. f	3. b 8. g
4. c 9. c	4. 4 9. 6	4. j 9. a	7–8. a, b	4. c 9. h	4. a 9. a	4. b 9. i	4. d 9. i
5. b 10. b	5. 9 10. 7	5. e 10. c	9–10. h, g	5. e 10. i	5. d 10. c	5. e 10. j	5. e 10. j

Chapter 12 (The People's Choice; The Christmas Wars)

Ten Words in Context	Matching Words with Definitions	Check 1	Check 2	Related Words	Word Work	Word Parts/Syn-Ant/Analogies	Final Check
1. b 5. a	1. 9 6. 3	1. j 6. c	1–2. f, d	1. b 6. j	1. a 6. b	1. c 6. c	1. e 6. f
2. a 6. c	2. 4 7. 7	2. a 7. h	3–4. c, a	2. a 7. f	2. e 7. a	2. c 7. b	2. c 7. i
3. c 7. b	3. 6 8. 2	3. d 8. g	5–6. j, h	3. e 8. g	3. b 8. b	3. d 8. d	3. b 8. g
4. c 8. a	4. 5 9. 8	4. f 9. i	7–8. i, e	4. d 9. i	4. c 9. b	4. a 9. a	4. d 9. j
5. b 10. c	5. 10 10. 1	5. b 10. e	9–10. g, b	5. c 10. h	5. d 10. c	5. c 10. b	5. a 10. h

Chapter 13 (What's Your Type?; What a Circus!)

Ten Words in Context	Matching Words with Definitions	Check 1	Check 2	Related Words	Word Work	Word Parts/Syn-Ant/Analogies	Final Check
1. c 6. c	1. 9 6. 2	1. j 6. h	1–2. i, h	1. e 6. h	1. a 6. c	1. b 6. j	1. e 6. j
2. a 7. a	2. 8 7. 4	2. a 7. c	3–4. e, f	2. b 7. f	2. a 7. a	2. c 7. g	2. c 7. i
3. a 8. b	3. 1 8. 6	3. f 8. d	5–6. d, a	3. a 8. j	3. c 8. c	3. e 8. i	3. d 8. g
4. c 9. a	4. 10 9. 5	4. i 9. g	7–8. c, b	4. d 9. g	4. c 9. b	4. d 9. h	4. b 9. f
5. b 10. c	5. 3 10. 7	5. b 10. e	9–10. j, g	5. c 10. i	5. b 10. b	5. a 10. f	5. a 10. h

Chapter 14 (Practicing Kindness; The Stinking Rose)

Ten Words in Context	Matching Words with Definitions	Check 1	Check 2	Related Words	Word Work	Word Parts/Syn-Ant/Analogies	Final Check
1. c 6. b	1. 9 6. 10	1. b 6. c	1–2. g, c	1. e 6. g	1. b 6. i	1. b 6. b	1. d 6. h
2. a 7. c	2. 1 7. 7	2. i 7. f	3–4. a, i	2. c 7. h	2. a 7. f	2. a 7. d	2. e 7. f
3. c 8. a	3. 8 8. 5	3. d 8. j	5–6. d, e	3. a 8. i	3. e 8. h	3. c 8. a	3. c 8. g
4. b 9. b	4. 4 9. 2	4. e 9. g	7–8. f, h	4. d 9. j	4. d 9. g	4. d 9. d	4. a 9. j
5. a 10. a	5. 3 10. 6	5. h 10. a	9–10. j, b	5. b 10. f	5. c 10. j	5. b 10. d	5. b 10. i

Chapter 15 (A Modern Fairy Tale; Wolf Children)

Ten Words in Context	Matching Words with Definitions	Check 1	Check 2	Related Words	Word Work	Word Parts/Syn-Ant/Analogies	Final Check
1. c 6. a	1. 9 6. 7	1. i 6. j	1–2. b, a	1. d 6. g	1. c 6. c	1. b 6. c	1. d 6. f
2. a 7. b	2. 4 7. 8	2. a 7. h	3–4. d, e	2. a 7. h	2. a 7. a	2. c 7. d	2. a 7. h
3. a 8. c	3. 10 8. 2	3. g 8. d	5–6. g, j	3. b 8. i	3. b 8. c	3. c 8. a	3. c 8. i
4. b 9. b	4. 5 9. 3	4. c 9. f	7–8. f, h	4. c 9. f	4. d 9. b	4. c 9. b	4. b 9. g
5. c 10. a	5. 6 10. 1	5. e 10. b	9–10. c, i	5. e 10. j	5. e 10. a	5. d 10. b	5. e 10. j

Chapter 16 (A Mismatched Couple; A Campaign to Become Class President)

Ten Words in Context	Matching Words with Definitions	Check 1	Check 2	Related Words	Word Work	Word Parts/Syn-Ant/Analogies	Final Check
1. b 6. b	1. 4 6. 6	1. j 6. a	1–2. j, i	1. d 6. g	1. c 6. c	1. a 6. f	1. b 6. i
2. a 7. c	2. 10 7. 3	2. c 7. f	3–4. b, h	2. b 7. f	2. a 7. b	2. d 7. j	2. c 7. g
3. c 8. c	3. 2 8. 1	3. g 8. h	5–6. d, f	3. e 8. h	3. d 8. a	3. c 8. i	3. a 8. j
4. b 9. a	4. 7 9. 8	4. e 9. d	7–8. a, c	4. a 9. i	4. e 9. c	4. b 9. h	4. d 9. f
5. c 10. b	5. 9 10. 5	5. i 10. b	9–10. g, e	5. c 10. j	5. b 10. b	5. e 10. g	5. e 10. h

Chapter 17 (The Famous Detective; Why So Quiet?)

Ten Words in Context	Matching Words with Definitions	Check 1	Check 2	Related Words	Word Work	Word Parts/Syn-Ant/Analogies	Final Check
1. c 6. a	1. 3 6. 9	1. a 6. h	1–2. g, h	1. b 6. h	1. d 6. c	1. d 6. b	1. c 6. h
2. b 7. b	2. 2 7. 7	2. d 7. i	3–4. j, i	2. c 7. f	2. b 7. a	2. b 7. c	2. a 7. f
3. b 8. a	3. 5 8. 1	3. c 8. e	5–6. c, b	3. d 8. i	3. a 8. c	3. a 8. a	3. b 8. i
4. c 9. b	4. 6 9. 4	4. b 9. g	7–8. e, d	4. e 9. j	4. e 9. b	4. c 9. c	4. d 9. g
5. c 10. b	5. 10 10. 8	5. j 10. f	9–10. f, a	5. a 10. g	5. c 10. c	5. c 10. c	5. e 10. i

Chapter 18 (Fear of Speaking; Do You Believe in Magic?)

Ten Words in Context	Matching Words with Definitions	Check 1	Check 2	Related Words	Word Work	Word Parts/Syn-Ant/Analogies	Final Check
1. c 6. a	1. 1 6. 9	1. f 6. b	1–2. f, g	1. d 6. g	1. c 6. b	1. d 6. h	1. e 6. h
2. b 7. a	2. 10 7. 7	2. c 7. h	3–4. h, c	2. b 7. h	2. c 7. a	2. b 7. i	2. b 7. f
3. b 8. c	3. 6 8. 4	3. a 8. e	5–6. b, a	3. a 8. f	3. c 8. b	3. a 8. f	3. c 8. j
4. c 9. b	4. 2 9. 3	4. i 9. j	7–8. d, i	4. e 9. i	4. a 9. c	4. c 9. g	4. a 9. i
5. b 10. a	5. 5 10. 8	5. g 10. d	9–10. e, j	5. c 10. j	5. b 10. a	5. e 10. j	5. d 10. g

Chapter 19 (The Miracle Runner; One of Those Days)

Ten Words in Context	Matching Words with Definitions	Check 1	Check 2	Related Words	Word Work	Word Parts/Syn-Ant/Analogies	Final Check
1. c 6. a	1. 9 6. 2	1. b 6. a	1–2. c, a	1. d 6. h	1. b 6. d	1. a 6. b	1. e 6. j
2. c 7. a	2. 8 7. 7	2. i 7. d	3–4. f, g	2. a 7. f	2. a 7. b	2. a 7. a	2. c 7. i
3. a 8. d	3. 1 8. 5	3. g 8. c	5–6. j, b	3. c 8. g	3. c 8. c	3. d 8. c	3. d 8. g
4. b 9. d	4. 4 9. 3	4. j 9. f	7–8. i, d	4. b 9. j	4. c 9. a	4. c 9. c	4. a 9. f
5. b 10. c	5. 6 10. 10	5. h 10. e	9–10. h, e	5. e 10. i	5. b 10. c	5. d 10. b	5. b 10. h

Chapter 20 (Pregnancy and Alcohol; A Criminal with a Tail)

Ten Words in Context	Matching Words with Definitions	Check 1	Check 2	Related Words	Word Work	Word Parts/Syn-Ant/Analogies	Final Check
1. b 6. a	1. 8 6. 5	1. e 6. f	1–2. i, h	1. b 6. h	1. b 6. c	1. d 6. a	1. c 6. j
2. a 7. b	2. 2 7. 6	2. h 7. g	3–4. j, c	2. e 7. i	2. a 7. a	2. b 7. d	2. a 7. i
3. c 8. a	3. 1 8. 10	3. c 8. b	5–6. b, e	3. d 8. g	3. c 8. d	3. a 8. b	3. e 8. f
4. a 9. b	4. 3 9. 9	4. d 9. i	7–8. g, d	4. a 9. f	4. b 9. e	4. c 9. b	4. d 9. h
5. c 10. b	5. 7 10. 4	5. j 10. a	9–10. a, f	5. c 10. j	5. c 10. b	5. d 10. d	5. b 10. g

Chapter 21 (Traveling with Children; Saving Earth's Natural Supplies)

Ten Words in Context	Matching Words with Definitions	Check 1	Check 2	Related Words	Word Work	Word Parts/Syn-Ant/Analogies	Final Check
1. a 6. b	1. 5 6. 6	1. e 6. i	1–2. a, f	1. d 6. h	1. a 6. c	1. e 6. h	1. e 6. i
2. a 7. c	2. 4 7. 9	2. h 7. c	3–4. j, c	2. c 7. f	2. b 7. a	2. a 7. g	2. a 7. h
3. b 8. a	3. 10 8. 7	3. a 8. g	5–6. g, h	3. b 8. g	3. c 8. b	3. d 8. j	3. d 8. f
4. c 9. b	4. 1 9. 2	4. j 9. d	7–8. b, d	4. e 9. j	4. a 9. b	4. c 9. i	4. c 9. j
5. c 10. c	5. 8 10. 3	5. b 10. f	9–10. e, i	5. a 10. i	5. b 10. c	5. b 10. f	5. b 10. g

Chapter 22 (More Fat, Anyone?; Is Prison Effective?)

Ten Words in Context		Matching Words with Definitions		Check 1		Check 2	Related Words		Word Work		Word Parts/Syn-Ant/Analogies		Final Check	
1. b	6. c	1. 4	6. 1	1. g	6. j	1–2. i, f	1. c	6. h	1. a	6. a	1. a	6. c	1. c	6. i
2. a	7. a	2. 3	7. 7	2. f	7. b	3–4. h, a	2. b	7. f	2. c	7. c	2. b	7. a	2. e	7. j
3. c	8. b	3. 6	8. 9	3. c	8. h	5–6. j, c	3. e	8. g	3. c	8. a	3. d	8. d	3. a	8. g
4. c	9. c	4. 2	9. 10	4. d	9. i	7–8. b, d	4. d	9. i	4. b	9. c	4. d	9. b	4. d	9. f
5. a	10. c	5. 8	10. 5	5. e	10. a	9–10. e, g	5. a	10. j	5. a	10. b	5. c	10. d	5. b	10. h

Chapter 23 (She Changed My Mind; So Sue Me)

Ten Words in Context		Matching Words with Definitions		Check 1		Check 2	Related Words		Word Work		Word Parts/Syn-Ant/Analogies		Final Check	
1. c	6. c	1. 7	6. 1	1. b	6. g	1–2. e, f	1. d	6. g	1. a	6. b	1. c	6. h	1. c	6. h
2. a	7. b	2. 8	7. 3	2. a	7. h	3–4. h, g	2. c	7. f	2. c	7. a	2. a	7. j	2. e	7. i
3. b	8. b	3. 2	8. 10	3. i	8. e	5–6. b, c	3. a	8. j	3. c	8. c	3. b	8. g	3. b	8. f
4. a	9. c	4. 6	9. 9	4. c	9. f	7–8. a, d	4. b	9. h	4. b	9. c	4. d	9. i	4. d	9. j
5. b	10. c	5. 5	10. 4	5. d	10. j	9–10. i, j	5. e	10. i	5. b	10. c	5. e	10. f	5. a	10. g

Chapter 24 (Fear of Public Speaking; Mrs. Thornton's Condition)

Ten Words in Context		Matching Words with Definitions		Check 1		Check 2	Related Words		Word Work		Word Parts/Syn-Ant/Analogies		Final Check	
1. b	6. a	1. 5	6. 1	1. b	6. a	1–2. d, g	1. d	6. h	1. d	6. b	1. c	6. a	1. a	6. i
2. c	7. c	2. 8	7. 4	2. h	7. d	3–4. a, b	2. a	7. i	2. a	7. a	2. b	7. d	2. e	7. g
3. b	8. b	3. 10	8. 7	3. g	8. e	5–6. e, f	3. c	8. f	3. e	8. b	3. c	8. d	3. c	8. j
4. c	9. b	4. 2	9. 3	4. i	9. c	7–8. c, h	4. b	9. g	4. c	9. c	4. a	9. c	4. d	9. f
5. b	10. b	5. 6	10. 9	5. j	10. f	9–10. i, j	5. e	10. j	5. b	10. b	5. c	10. d	5. b	10. h

Chapter 25 (Wacky Weddings; The Cost of Hatred)

Ten Words in Context		Matching Words with Definitions		Check 1		Check 2	Related Words		Word Work		Word Parts/Syn-Ant/Analogies		Final Check	
1. b	6. a	1. 3	6. 7	1. d	6. g	1–2. a, j	1. b	6. h	1. c	6. a	1. b	6. a	1. c	6. j
2. a	7. a	2. 2	7. 9	2. b	7. f	3–4. h, b	2. c	7. g	2. b	7. b	2. d	7. c	2. b	7. h
3. b	8. c	3. 1	8. 10	3. c	8. h	5–6. f, c	3. d	8. f	3. c	8. d	3. a	8. d	3. d	8. f
4. c	9. b	4. 5	9. 8	4. a	9. e	7–8. i, d	4. e	9. j	4. a	9. e	4. d	9. b	4. a	9. g
5. c	10. b	5. 4	10. 6	5. i	10. j	9–10. g, e	5. a	10. i	5. b	10. c	5. d	10. b	5. e	10. i

Pretest

NAME: _____

SECTION: _____ DATE: _____

SCORE: _____

This test contains 100 items. In the space provided, write the letter of the choice that is closest in meaning to the **boldfaced** word.

Important: Keep in mind that this test is for diagnostic purposes only. **If you do not know a word, leave the space blank rather than guess at it.**

_____ 1. To **communicate** is to: **a**) anger   **b**) inform   **c**) hurry   **d**) mistake

_____ 2. If you **deceive**, you: **a**) mislead   **b**) encourage   **c**) prevent   **d**) forbid

_____ 3. An **earnest** person is: **a**) dishonest   **b**) wealthy   **c**) unpleasant   **d**) sincere

_____ 4. A story that is **fiction** is: **a**) made up   **b**) exciting   **c**) violent   **d**) romantic

_____ 5. A **theory** is a(n):   **a**) opportunity   **b**) unproven explanation   **c**) certainty   **d**) excuse

_____ 6. To **determine** is to: **a**) suspect   **b**) find out   **c**) persuade   **d**) compliment

_____ 7. To **dispose of** is to: **a**) throw away   **b**) ignore   **c**) keep   **d**) repeat

_____ 8. Something that is **evident** is: **a**) hidden   **b**) frightening   **c**) obvious   **d**) musical

_____ 9. To **preserve** is to: **a**) pretend   **b**) protect   **c**) absorb   **d**) expect

_____ 10. To **restore** is to: **a**) repair   **b**) destroy   **c**) bury   **d**) lift up

_____ 11. To **appeal** to is to: **a**) make a request   **b**) say no   **c**) take away the outside part   **d**) repeat

_____ 12. To **establish** is to: **a**) start   **b**) knock down   **c**) flatten   **d**) repeat

_____ 13. One's **potential** is one's: **a**) ancestors   **b**) age   **c**) possibility   **d**) preference

_____ 14. A **variety** is a(n):   **a**) opinion   **b**) mixture   **c**) reason   **d**) delay

_____ 15. Something **wholesome** is: **a**) healthful   **b**) disgusting   **c**) foreign   **d**) childlike

_____ 16. To **possess** is to: **a**) plan   **b**) adjust   **c**) leave unchanged   **d**) own

_____ 17. A **procedure** is a(n):   **a**) method   **b**) opinion   **c**) public   **d**) piece of property

_____ 18. To **renew** is to: **a**) find   **b**) make active again   **c**) force one's will upon   **d**) attempt

_____ 19. **Resources** are: **a**) supplies   **b**) costs   **c**) responses   **d**) agreements

_____ 20. To be **sufficient** is to be: **a**) less than is needed   **b**) humorous   **c**) empty   **d**) enough

_____ 21. To **assume** is to: **a**) suppose to be true   **b**) prove to be false   **c**) not care   **d**) argue for

_____ 22. To **exhaust** is to: **a**) refill   **b**) remove from sight   **c**) use up   **d**) fall

_____ 23. The **maximum** amount is: **a**) the worst   **b**) the most   **c**) the lightest   **d**) the least

_____ 24. An **objective** is a(n):   **a**) bad influence   **b**) reason to believe   **c**) insult   **d**) goal

_____ 25. To **protest** is to: **a**) speak out against   **b**) encourage   **c**) prove   **d**) test

(Continues on next page)

Copyright © 1998 by Townsend Press. Permission to copy this test is granted to teachers using *Groundwork for a Better Vocabulary* as a class text.

_____ 26. If you are **anxious**, you are: **a)** sleepy   **b)** young   **c)** busy   **d)** worried

_____ 27. To **convince** is to: **a)** cause to believe   **b)** refuse to accept   **c)** disregard   **d)** clean up

_____ 28. An **inferior** product is: **a)** highly valued   **b)** poor in quality   **c)** heavy
   d) unbreakable

_____ 29. To **overwhelm** is to: **a)** dissolve   **b)** understand   **c)** make helpless   **d)** make whole

_____ 30. A **thorough** job is: **a)** carefully done   **b)** wasted   **c)** forgotten   **d)** well-paying

_____ 31. To be **current** is to be: **a)** modern   **b)** few in number   **c)** good tasting   **d)** likable

_____ 32. To **maintain** is to: **a)** release from captivity   **b)** keep in existence
   c) prove to be correct   **d)** admire

_____ 33. A **minimum** number is: **a)** the largest possible   **b)** desirable   **c)** the smallest possible
   d) more than expected

_____ 34. To **originate** is to: **a)** imitate   **b)** begin   **c)** impress   **d)** pretend

_____ 35. To be **reliable** is to be: **a)** untrustworthy   **b)** easily tricked   **c)** dependable   **d)** healthy

_____ 36. To be **conscious** is to be: **a)** drowsy   **b)** awake   **c)** depressed   **d)** purposeful

_____ 37. Something **external** is: **a)** buried deeply   **b)** on the outside   **c)** unimportant   **d)** helpful

_____ 38. To be **incredible** is to be: **a)** unbelievable   **b)** showy   **c)** humble   **d)** wasteful

_____ 39. **Internal** means: **a)** inner   **b)** uncommon   **c)** easy   **d)** understood by few

_____ 40. A **remedy** is a(n):   **a)** source of amusement   **b)** usual manner of doing something
   c) collection of writings   **d)** cure

_____ 41. **Appropriate** actions are: **a)** rude   **b)** impulsive   **c)** unwise   **d)** proper

_____ 42. To **bewilder** is to: **a)** calm   **b)** confuse   **c)** accept   **d)** explain

_____ 43. **Emotion** is: **a)** feeling   **b)** eyesight   **c)** movement   **d)** payment

_____ 44. To **investigate** is to: **a)** abandon   **b)** make secure   **c)** examine   **d)** insist

_____ 45. To be **legible** is to be: **a)** heavy   **b)** clear   **c)** empty   **d)** noisy

_____ 46. To **analyze** is to: **a)** disturb   **b)** get rid of (something)   **c)** dislike   **d)** examine

_____ 47. A **category** is a(n):   **a)** group of similar things   **b)** means of expression
   c) lack of understanding   **d)** denial

_____ 48. One who is **critical** is: **a)** well-liked   **b)** disapproving   **c)** lacking intelligence
   d) not taking sides in a quarrel

_____ 49. A **deliberate** act is: **a)** done on purpose   **b)** unwise   **c)** amazing   **d)** criminal

_____ 50. **Frustration** is: **a)** great delight   **b)** discouragement   **c)** cruelty   **d)** luck

(Continues on next page)

_____ 51. To be **accustomed to** is to be: **a**) unused to **b**) in the habit of **c**) unable to **d**) angry at

_____ 52. To **misinterpret** is to: **a**) have respect **b**) prefer **c**) understand incorrectly **d**) get rid of

_____ 53. To **occur** is to: **a**) disappear **b**) repeat **c**) respond **d**) happen

_____ 54. When you **revise**, you: **a**) correct and improve **b**) discard **c**) copy without giving credit **d**) fail to complete

_____ 55. A **version** is a: **a**) report based on one point of view **b**) poem **c**) hatred **d**) deliberately mean remark

_____ 56. A **conflict** is a(n): **a**) period of time **b**) point of view **c**) lesson **d**) disagreement

_____ 57. **Stress** is: **a**) tension **b**) relaxation **c**) enjoyment **d**) excitement

_____ 58. A **unanimous** decision is: **a**) poorly thought out **b**) mixed **c**) based on complete agreement **d**) mistaken

_____ 59. To **vary** is to: **a**) change **b**) insist **c**) remain the same **d**) recognize

_____ 60. A **vicinity** is a(n): **a**) heated argument **b**) area around a place **c**) written pamphlet **d**) type of lamp

_____ 61. A **burden** is a(n): **a**) hardship **b**) joy **c**) reply **d**) payment

_____ 62. To be **economical** is to be: **a**) wasteful **b**) rich **c**) thrifty **d**) forgiving

_____ 63. An **extravagant** person is: **a**) critical **b**) wasteful **c**) wise **d**) messy

_____ 64. **Security** is: **a**) protection **b**) loneliness **c**) immaturity **d**) ridicule

_____ 65. To **sympathize** is to: **a**) share feeling **b**) object **c**) refuse **d**) avoid

_____ 66. To **coincide** is to: **a**) remove from consideration **b**) happen at the same time **c**) make clear **d**) read carefully

_____ 67. A **considerable** size is: **a**) rather small **b**) too small **c**) too large **d**) rather large

_____ 68. An **intentional** act is: **a**) on purpose **b**) accidental **c**) misguided **d**) against the law

_____ 69. To be **unstable** is to be: **a**) usual **b**) strong **c**) unsteady **d**) complete

_____ 70. To **utilize** is to: **a**) suggest **b**) make use of **c**) control by force **d**) accept as fact

_____ 71. Something **artificial** is: **a**) natural **b**) impressive **c**) not natural **d**) worn out

_____ 72. **Frequency** means: **a**) how often something happens **b**) how fast something is **c**) how loud something is **d**) where something comes from

_____ 73. To **represent** is to: **a**) avoid talking about **b**) prefer **c**) be a symbol of **d**) allow to happen

_____ 74. Something **temporary** is: **a**) expected to last forever **b**) impossible to achieve **c**) serving for a limited time **d**) clearly seen

_____ 75. A **triumph** is a: **a**) victory **b**) defeat **c**) compromise **d**) battle

(Continues on next page)

_____ 76. An **attitude** is a:　　**a)** decrease　　**b)** success　　**c)** frame of mind　　**d)** height

_____ 77. A **contrast** is a:　　**a)** striking difference　　**b)** similarity　　**c)** suggestion　　**d)** bright color

_____ 78. To be **excessive** is to be:　　**a)** kindly　　**b)** slow to anger　　**c)** not enough　　**d)** too much

_____ 79. A **fragile** object is:　　**a)** expensive　　**b)** easily broken　　**c)** richly decorated　　**d)** tasteless

_____ 80. To **indicate** is to:　　**a)** pay attention to　　**b)** fail to see　　**c)** go in　　**d)** point out

_____ 81. An **emphasis** is a(n):　　**a)** refusal to speak　　**b)** betrayal　　**c)** importance given to something
d) stubborn act

_____ 82. To **interpret** is to:　　**a)** confuse　　**b)** make an effort　　**c)** light from within　　**d)** explain

_____ 83. To **propose** is to:　　**a)** persuade　　**b)** suggest　　**c)** exaggerate　　**d)** leave out

_____ 84. An **ultimate** experience is:　　**a)** common　　**b)** inefficient　　**c)** dangerous　　**d)** the greatest

_____ 85. To be **vague** is to be:　　**a)** unclear　　**b)** shining　　**c)** in fashion　　**d)** embarrassing

_____ 86. Something **apparent** is:　　**a)** impossible to see with the naked eye
b) made up of many small parts　　**c)** obvious　　**d)** hard to understand

_____ 87. If something is **automatic**, it:　　**a)** is easily moved　　**b)** operates by itself　　**c)** cannot change
d) improves over time

_____ 88. To **fulfill** is to:　　**a)** carry out　　**b)** fail at a task　　**c)** understand another's feelings
d) give advice

_____ 89. To **influence** is to:　　**a)** misunderstand　　**b)** excuse　　**c)** be offended　　**d)** persuade

_____ 90. To **transfer** is to:　　**a)** find fault　　**b)** discontinue　　**c)** send from one place to another
d) inspect

_____ 91. To **complicate** is to:　　**a)** smooth over　　**b)** adjust　　**c)** make difficult　　**d)** recognize

_____ 92. A **conscience** is a(n):　　**a)** sense of being awake　　**b)** inability to decide
c) sense of right and wrong　　**d)** skill with numbers

_____ 93. To **counsel** is to:　　**a)** improve　　**b)** approve　　**c)** give advice　　**d)** meet

_____ 94. To **detect** is to:　　**a)** get　　**b)** complain　　**c)** remark　　**d)** notice

_____ 95. To be **transparent** is to be:　　**a)** sent away　　**b)** dark in color　　**c)** seen through easily　　**d)** unusual

_____ 96. To **comprehend** is to:　　**a)** dislike　　**b)** repeat　　**c)** protect　　**d)** understand

_____ 97. Something **dramatic** is:　　**a)** impressive　　**b)** hard to notice　　**c)** odd　　**d)** boring

_____ 98. To be **frank** is to be:　　**a)** untruthful　　**b)** youthful　　**c)** honest　　**d)** painful

_____ 99. To **illustrate** is to:　　**a)** give an example　　**b)** destroy　　**c)** repair　　**d)** send off

_____ 100. An **impression** is a(n):　　**a)** lie　　**b)** iron　　**c)** opinion　　**d)** center (of something)

STOP. This is the end of the test. If there is time remaining, you may go back and recheck your answers. When the time is up, hand in both your answer sheet and this test booklet to your instructor.

GROUNDWORK FOR A
BETTER VOCABULARY
Posttest

NAME: _____

SECTION: _____ DATE: _____

SCORE: _____

> This test contains 100 items. In the space provided, write the letter of the choice that is closest in meaning to the **boldfaced** word.

_____ 1. To **determine** is to: **a)** suspect   **b)** persuade   **c)** find out   **d)** compliment

_____ 2. To **dispose of** is to: **a)** repeat   **b)** ignore   **c)** keep   **d)** throw away

_____ 3. Something that is **evident** is: **a)** hidden   **b)** obvious   **c)** musical   **d)** frightening

_____ 4. To **preserve** is to: **a)** pretend   **b)** expect   **c)** absorb   **d)** protect

_____ 5. To **restore** is to: **a)** destroy   **b)** repair   **c)** bury   **d)** lift up

_____ 6. To **possess** is to: **a)** plan   **b)** adjust   **c)** own   **d)** leave unchanged

_____ 7. A **procedure** is a(n):   **a)** public   **b)** opinion   **c)** method   **d)** piece of property

_____ 8. To **renew** is to: **a)** find   **b)** attempt   **c)** force one's will upon   **d)** make active again

_____ 9. **Resources** are: **a)** agreements   **b)** supplies   **c)** responses   **d)** costs

_____ 10. To be **sufficient** is to be: **a)** less than is needed   **b)** humorous   **c)** enough   **d)** empty

_____ 11. To **appeal** to is to: **a)** repeat   **b)** say no   **c)** take away the outside part   **d)** make a request

_____ 12. To **establish** is to: **a)** flatten   **b)** knock down   **c)** start   **d)** repeat

_____ 13. One's **potential** is one's: **a)** ancestors   **b)** possibility   **c)** age   **d)** preference

_____ 14. A **variety** is a(n):   **a)** opinion   **b)** delay   **c)** reason   **d)** mixture

_____ 15. Something **wholesome** is: **a)** foreign   **b)** disgusting   **c)** healthful   **d)** childlike

_____ 16. To **assume** is to: **a)** prove to be false   **b)** argue for   **c)** not care   **d)** suppose to be true

_____ 17. To **exhaust** is to: **a)** use up   **b)** remove from sight   **c)** refill   **d)** fall

_____ 18. The **maximum** amount is: **a)** the worst   **b)** the lightest   **c)** the most   **d)** the least

_____ 19. An **objective** is a(n):   **a)** bad influence   **b)** reason to believe   **c)** goal   **d)** insult

_____ 20. To **protest** is to: **a)** test   **b)** encourage   **c)** prove   **d)** speak out against

_____ 21. To **communicate** is to: **a)** anger   **b)** hurry   **c)** inform   **d)** mistake

_____ 22. If you **deceive**, you: **a)** encourage   **b)** mislead   **c)** prevent   **d)** forbid

_____ 23. An **earnest** person is: **a)** sincere   **b)** wealthy   **c)** unpleasant   **d)** dishonest

_____ 24. A story that is **fiction** is: **a)** violent   **b)** exciting   **c)** made up   **d)** romantic

_____ 25. A **theory** is a(n):   **a)** excuse   **b)** opportunity   **c)** certainty   **d)** unproven explanation

(Continues on next page)

_____ 26. To be **current** is to be: **a)** good tasting   **b)** few in number   **c)** modern   **d)** likable

_____ 27. To **maintain** is to: **a)** release from captivity   **b)** admire
   c) prove to be correct   **d)** keep in existence

_____ 28. A **minimum** number is: **a)** the smallest possible   **b)** desirable   **c)** the largest possible
   d) more than expected

_____ 29. To **originate** is to: **a)** begin   **b)** imitate   **c)** impress   **d)** pretend

_____ 30. To be **reliable** is to be: **a)** untrustworthy   **b)** dependable   **c)** easily tricked   **d)** healthy

_____ 31. **Appropriate** actions are: **a)** rude   **b)** impulsive   **c)** proper   **d)** unwise

_____ 32. To **bewilder** is to: **a)** confuse   **b)** calm   **c)** accept   **d)** explain

_____ 33. **Emotion** is: **a)** eyesight   **b)** feeling   **c)** movement   **d)** payment

_____ 34. To **investigate** is to: **a)** examine   **b)** make secure   **c)** abandon   **d)** insist

_____ 35. To be **legible** is to be: **a)** heavy   **b)** noisy   **c)** empty   **d)** clear

_____ 36. To **analyze** is to: **a)** disturb   **b)** get rid of (something)   **c)** examine   **d)** dislike

_____ 37. A **category** is a(n):   **a)** denial   **b)** means of expression   **c)** lack of understanding
   d) group of similar things

_____ 38. One who is **critical** is: **a)** well-liked   **b)** lacking intelligence
   c) not taking sides in a quarrel   **d)** disapproving

_____ 39. A **deliberate** act is: **a)** amazing   **b)** unwise   **c)** done on purpose   **d)** criminal

_____ 40. **Frustration** is: **a)** discouragement   **b)** great delight   **c)** cruelty   **d)** luck

_____ 41. If you are **anxious**, you are: **a)** sleepy   **b)** worried   **c)** busy   **d)** young

_____ 42. To **convince** is to: **a)** disregard   **b)** refuse to accept   **c)** cause to believe   **d)** clean up

_____ 43. An **inferior** product is: **a)** poor in quality   **b)** highly valued   **c)** heavy
   d) unbreakable

_____ 44. To **overwhelm** is to: **a)** dissolve   **b)** make helpless   **c)** understand   **d)** make whole

_____ 45. A **thorough** job is: **a)** forgotten   **b)** wasted   **c)** carefully done   **d)** well-paying

_____ 46. To be **conscious** is to be: **a)** drowsy   **b)** purposeful   **c)** depressed   **d)** awake

_____ 47. Something **external** is: **a)** buried deeply   **b)** helpful   **c)** unimportant   **d)** on the outside

_____ 48. To be **incredible** is to be: **a)** humble   **b)** showy   **c)** unbelievable   **d)** wasteful

_____ 49. **Internal** means: **a)** understood by few   **b)** uncommon   **c)** easy   **d)** inner

_____ 50. A **remedy** is a(n):   **a)** source of amusement   **b)** usual manner of doing something
   c) cure   **d)** collection of writings

(Continues on next page)

____ 51. Something **artificial** is: **a**) not natural   **b**) impressive   **c**) natural   **d**) worn out

____ 52. **Frequency** means: **a**) where something comes from   **b**) how fast something is
c) how loud something is   **d**) how often something happens

____ 53. To **represent** is to: **a**) avoid talking about   **b**) be a symbol of   **c**) prefer
d) allow to happen

____ 54. Something **temporary** is: **a**) serving for a limited time   **b**) impossible to achieve
c) expected to last forever   **d**) clearly seen

____ 55. A **triumph** is a: **a**) compromise   **b**) defeat   **c**) victory   **d**) battle

____ 56. To **coincide** is to: **a**) remove from consideration   **b**) read carefully
c) make clear   **d**) happen at the same time

____ 57. A **considerable** size is: **a**) rather small   **b**) too small   **c**) rather large   **d**) too large

____ 58. An **intentional** act is: **a**) accidental   **b**) on purpose   **c**) misguided   **d**) against the law

____ 59. To be **unstable** is to be: **a**) unsteady   **b**) strong   **c**) usual   **d**) complete

____ 60. To **utilize** is to: **a**) suggest   **b**) control by force   **c**) make use of   **d**) accept as fact

____ 61. A **burden** is a(n):   **a**) joy   **b**) hardship   **c**) reply   **d**) payment

____ 62. To be **economical** is to be: **a**) wasteful   **b**) rich   **c**) forgiving   **d**) thrifty

____ 63. An **extravagant** person is: **a**) critical   **b**) messy   **c**) wise   **d**) wasteful

____ 64. **Security** is: **a**) loneliness   **b**) protection   **c**) immaturity   **d**) ridicule

____ 65. To **sympathize** is to: **a**) avoid   **b**) object   **c**) refuse   **d**) share feeling

____ 66. A **conflict** is a(n):   **a**) period of time   **b**) disagreement   **c**) lesson   **d**) point of view

____ 67. **Stress** is: **a**) excitement   **b**) relaxation   **c**) enjoyment   **d**) tension

____ 68. A **unanimous** decision is: **a**) based on complete agreement   **b**) mixed   **c**) poorly thought out
d) mistaken

____ 69. To **vary** is to: **a**) insist   **b**) change   **c**) remain the same   **d**) recognize

____ 70. A **vicinity** is a(n):   **a**) heated argument   **b**) type of lamp   **c**) written pamphlet
d) area around a place

____ 71. To be **accustomed to** is to be: **a**) unused to   **b**) unable to   **c**) in the habit of   **d**) angry at

____ 72. To **misinterpret** is to: **a**) have respect   **b**) prefer   **c**) get rid of   **d**) understand incorrectly

____ 73. To **occur** is to: **a**) disappear   **b**) happen   **c**) respond   **d**) repeat

____ 74. When you **revise**, you: **a**) copy without giving credit   **b**) discard   **c**) correct and improve
d) fail to complete

____ 75. A **version** is a: **a**) deliberately mean remark   **b**) poem   **c**) hatred
d) report based on one point of view

(Continues on next page)

_____ 76. Something **apparent** is: **a**) made up of many small parts   **b**) obvious
       c) impossible to see with the naked eye   **d**) hard to understand

_____ 77. If something is **automatic**, it: **a**) is easily moved   **b**) improves over time   **c**) cannot change
       d) operates by itself

_____ 78. To **fulfill** is to: **a**) carry out   **b**) fail at a task   **c**) understand another's feelings
       d) give advice

_____ 79. To **influence** is to: **a**) misunderstand   **b**) be offended   **c**) persuade   **d**) excuse

_____ 80. To **transfer** is to: **a**) inspect   **b**) discontinue   **c**) find fault
       d) send from one place to another

_____ 81. To **complicate** is to: **a**) smooth over   **b**) adjust   **c**) recognize   **d**) make difficult

_____ 82. A **conscience** is a(n):   **a**) sense of being awake   **b**) sense of right and wrong
       c) inability to decide   **d**) skill with numbers

_____ 83. To **counsel** is to: **a**) improve   **b**) give advice   **c**) approve   **d**) meet

_____ 84. To **detect** is to: **a**) get   **b**) complain   **c**) notice   **d**) remark

_____ 85. To be **transparent** is to be: **a**) seen through easily   **b**) dark in color   **c**) sent away   **d**) unusual

_____ 86. An **attitude** is a: **a**) decrease   **b**) frame of mind   **c**) success   **d**) height

_____ 87. A **contrast** is a: **a**) bright color   **b**) similarity   **c**) suggestion   **d**) striking difference

_____ 88. To be **frank** is to be: **a**) honest   **b**) youthful   **c**) untruthful   **d**) painful

_____ 89. A **fragile** object is: **a**) expensive   **b**) tasteless   **c**) richly decorated   **d**) easily broken

_____ 90. An **impression** is a(n):   **a**) lie   **b**) opinion   **c**) iron   **d**) center (of something)

_____ 91. An **emphasis** is a(n):   **a**) refusal to speak   **b**) betrayal   **c**) stubborn act
       d) importance given to something

_____ 92. To **interpret** is to: **a**) confuse   **b**) make an effort   **c**) explain   **d**) light from within

_____ 93. To **propose** is to: **a**) suggest   **b**) persuade   **c**) exaggerate   **d**) leave out

_____ 94. An **ultimate** experience is: **a**) common   **b**) inefficient   **c**) the greatest   **d**) dangerous

_____ 95. To be **vague** is to be: **a**) shining   **b**) unclear   **c**) in fashion   **d**) embarrassing

_____ 96. To **comprehend** is to: **a**) dislike   **b**) understand   **c**) protect   **d**) repeat

_____ 97. Something **dramatic** is: **a**) odd   **b**) hard to notice   **c**) impressive   **d**) boring

_____ 98. To be **excessive** is to be: **a**) too much   **b**) slow to anger   **c**) not enough   **d**) kindly

_____ 99. To **illustrate** is to: **a**) destroy   **b**) give an example   **c**) repair   **d**) send off

_____ 100. To **indicate** is to: **a**) point out   **b**) fail to see   **c**) go in   **d**) pay attention to

STOP. This is the end of the test. If there is time remaining, you may go back and recheck your answers. When the time is up, hand in both your answer sheet and this test booklet to your instructor.

Name: _____

Unit 1: *Pretest*

In the space provided, write the letter of the choice that is closest in meaning to the **boldfaced** word.

_____ 1. **challenge**   **a)** a piece of sporting equipment   **b)** something requiring extra effort
     c) an untrue and malicious story   **d)** a source of pain

_____ 2. **dependent**   **a)** refusing aid   **b)** relying on others   **c)** easily angered   **d)** unable to read

_____ 3. **fertile**   **a)** alone   **b)** definite   **c)** productive   **d)** shy

_____ 4. **peculiar**   **a)** friendly   **b)** highly skilled   **c)** violent   **d)** odd

_____ 5. **preference**   **a)** expression of dislike   **b)** form of punishment   **c)** suggestion
     d) first choice

_____ 6. **principal**   **a)** most important   **b)** small in number   **c)** physically large   **d)** purposeful

_____ 7. **solitary**   **a)** full of life   **b)** alone   **c)** clever   **d)** whole

_____ 8. **suitable**   **a)** proper   **b)** well-dressed   **c)** filled with regret   **d)** absent

_____ 9. **surplus**   **a)** insufficient   **b)** ruined   **c)** extra   **d)** planned

_____ 10. **transform**   **a)** change   **b)** remain the same   **c)** frighten   **d)** create

_____ 11. **analyze**   **a)** disturb   **b)** get rid of (something)   **c)** dislike   **d)** examine

_____ 12. **attitude**   **a)** decrease   **b)** success   **c)** frame of mind   **d)** dislike

_____ 13. **category**   **a)** group with characteristics in common   **b)** means of expression
     c) lack of understanding   **d)** denial

_____ 14. **contrast**   **a)** striking difference   **b)** similarity   **c)** suggestion   **d)** bright color

_____ 15. **critical**   **a)** well-liked   **b)** disapproving   **c)** lacking intelligence   **d)** not taking

_____ 16. **deliberate**   **a)** done on purpose   **b)** unwise   **c)** amazing   **d)** criminal

_____ 17. **excessive**   **a)** kindly   **b)** slow to anger   **c)** not enough   **d)** too much

_____ 18. **fragile**   **a)** poorly made   **b)** easily broken   **c)** richly decorated   **d)** tasteless

_____ 19. **frustration**   **a)** great delight   **b)** discouragement   **c)** cruelty   **d)** luck

_____ 20. **indicate**   **a)** pay attention (to)   **b)** fail to see   **c)** object (to)   **d)** point out

_____ 21. **accompany**   **a)** abandon   **b)** meet unexpectedly   **c)** receive   **d)** go along with

_____ 22. **desperate**   **a)** in great need   **b)** content   **c)** furious   **d)** sorrowful

_____ 23. **determine**   **a)** suspect   **b)** find out   **c)** persuade   **d)** compliment

_____ 24. **dispose of**   **a)** throw away   **b)** ignore   **c)** silence   **d)** repeat

_____ 25. **evident**   **a)** hidden   **b)** brightly colored   **c)** obvious   **d)** musical

(Continues on next page)

____ 26. **preserve**	a) pretend b) protect c) absorb d) expect	
____ 27. **pursue**	a) capture b) chase c) control d) rest	
____ 28. **rejection**	a) invitation b) action c) possibility d) refusal	
____ 29. **restore**	a) repair b) destroy c) bury d) lift up	
____ 30. **scarce**	a) in great amount b) not needed c) hard to find d) empty	
____ 31. **abundant**	a) quickly used up b) unwanted c) overpriced d) more than enough	
____ 32. **betray**	a) cooperate with b) allow to happen c) be disloyal to d) weigh down	
____ 33. **comparison**	a) act of considering how two things are similar or different b) sense of freedom from danger c) type of literature made of imaginary events d) belief based upon little information	
____ 34. **demonstrate**	a) explain by showing b) break into pieces c) bury d) have complete knowledge of	
____ 35. **dispute**	a) formal agreement b) sense of hopelessness c) quarrel d) opinion	
____ 36. **distinct**	a) shady b) without value c) able to produce offspring d) obvious	
____ 37. **exaggerate**	a) overstate b) lessen in size c) state the truth d) avoid	
____ 38. **inhabit**	a) put to good use b) serve as a substitute for c) make up d) live in	
____ 39. **neutral**	a) changing one's opinion readily b) refusing to take sides in a quarrel c) discovering the truth d) acting against one's stated beliefs	
____ 40. **reduction**	a) shipment b) explanation c) decrease d) correction	
____ 41. **aggravate**	a) improve b) correct c) ignore d) make worse	
____ 42. **cease**	a) continue b) prepare c) stop d) allow	
____ 43. **coincide**	a) remove from consideration b) happen at the same time c) make clear d) read carefully	
____ 44. **considerable**	a) less than expected b) heartless c) impossible d) large	
____ 45. **humane**	a) kind b) absent-minded c) cruel d) talented	
____ 46. **intentional**	a) on purpose b) accidental c) misguided d) against the law	
____ 47. **interference**	a) sudden quiet b) loss of heat c) getting in the way d) acceptance	
____ 48. **obnoxious**	a) well-meaning b) unpleasant c) comical d) unclear	
____ 49. **unstable**	a) usual b) strong c) unsteady d) complete	
____ 50. **utilize**	a) suggest b) make use of c) control by force d) accept as fact	

SCORE: (Number correct) _____ × 2 = _____ %

Name: _____

Unit 1: *Posttest*

In the space provided, write the letter of the choice that is closest in meaning to the **boldfaced** word.

_____ 1. **analyze**　　**a)** examine　**b)** get rid of (something)　**c)** dislike　**d)** disturb

_____ 2. **attitude**　　**a)** decrease　**b)** frame of mind　**c)** success　**d)** dislike

_____ 3. **category**　　**a)** denial　**b)** means of expression
　　　　　　　　　c) lack of understanding　**d)** group with characteristics in common

_____ 4. **contrast**　　**a)** suggestion　**b)** similarity　**c)** striking difference　**d)** bright color

_____ 5. **critical**　　**a)** well-liked　**b)** not taking　**c)** lacking intelligence　**d)** disapproving

_____ 6. **principal**　　**a)** physically large　**b)** small in number　**c)** most important　**d)** purposeful

_____ 7. **solitary**　　**a)** alone　**b)** full of life　**c)** clever　**d)** whole

_____ 8. **suitable**　　**a)** well-dressed　**b)** proper　**c)** filled with regret　**d)** absent

_____ 9. **surplus**　　**a)** insufficient　**b)** ruined　**c)** planned　**d)** extra

_____ 10. **transform**　　**a)** frighten　**b)** remain the same　**c)** change　**d)** create

_____ 11. **accompany**　　**a)** abandon　**b)** meet unexpectedly　**c)** go along with　**d)** receive

_____ 12. **desperate**　　**a)** content　**b)** in great need　**c)** furious　**d)** sorrowful

_____ 13. **determine**　　**a)** suspect　**b)** persuade　**c)** find out　**d)** compliment

_____ 14. **dispose of**　　**a)** repeat　**b)** ignore　**c)** silence　**d)** throw away

_____ 15. **evident**　　**a)** hidden　**b)** obvious　**c)** brightly colored　**d)** musical

_____ 16. **deliberate**　　**a)** amazing　**b)** unwise　**c)** done on purpose　**d)** criminal

_____ 17. **excessive**　　**a)** too much　**b)** slow to anger　**c)** not enough　**d)** kindly

_____ 18. **fragile**　　**a)** poorly made　**b)** richly decorated　**c)** easily broken　**d)** tasteless

_____ 19. **frustration**　　**a)** discouragement　**b)** great delight　**c)** cruelty　**d)** luck

_____ 20. **indicate**　　**a)** pay attention (to)　**b)** fail to see　**c)** point out　**d)** object (to)

_____ 21. **challenge**　　**a)** something requiring extra effort　**b)** a piece of sporting equipment
　　　　　　　　　c) an untrue and malicious story　**d)** a source of pain

_____ 22. **dependent**　　**a)** relying on others　**b)** refusing aid　**c)** easily angered　**d)** unable to read

_____ 23. **fertile**　　**a)** alone　**b)** definite　**c)** shy　**d)** productive

_____ 24. **peculiar**　　**a)** friendly　**b)** odd　**c)** violent　**d)** highly skilled

_____ 25. **preference**　　**a)** expression of dislike　**b)** form of punishment　**c)** first choice
　　　　　　　　　d) suggestion

(Continues on next page)

_____ 26. **preserve** **a)** pretend **b)** expect **c)** absorb **d)** protect

_____ 27. **pursue** **a)** chase **b)** capture **c)** control **d)** rest

_____ 28. **rejection** **a)** invitation **b)** action **c)** refusal **d)** possibility

_____ 29. **restore** **a)** destroy **b)** repair **c)** bury **d)** lift up

_____ 30. **scarce** **a)** hard to find **b)** not needed **c)** in great amount **d)** empty

_____ 31. **abundant** **a)** quickly used up **b)** more than enough **c)** overpriced **d)** unwanted

_____ 32. **betray** **a)** cooperate with **b)** be disloyal to **c)** allow to happen **d)** weigh down

_____ 33. **comparison** **a)** belief based upon little information **b)** sense of freedom from danger
c) type of literature made of imaginary events
d) act of considering how two things are similar or different

_____ 34. **demonstrate** **a)** bury **b)** break into pieces **c)** explain by showing
d) have complete knowledge of

_____ 35. **dispute** **a)** formal agreement **b)** sense of hopelessness **c)** opinion **d)** quarrel

_____ 36. **distinct** **a)** obvious **b)** without value **c)** able to produce offspring **d)** shady

_____ 37. **exaggerate** **a)** lessen in size **b)** overstate **c)** state the truth **d)** avoid

_____ 38. **inhabit** **a)** put to good use **b)** serve as a substitute for **c)** live in **d)** make up

_____ 39. **neutral** **a)** changing one's opinion readily **b)** acting against one's stated beliefs
c) discovering the truth **d)** refusing to take sides in a quarrel

_____ 40. **reduction** **a)** decrease **b)** explanation **c)** shipment **d)** correction

_____ 41. **aggravate** **a)** improve **b)** correct **c)** make worse **d)** ignore

_____ 42. **cease** **a)** continue **b)** stop **c)** prepare **d)** allow

_____ 43. **coincide** **a)** remove from consideration **b)** make clear **c)** happen at the same time
d) read carefully

_____ 44. **considerable** **a)** less than expected **b)** large **c)** impossible **d)** heartless

_____ 45. **humane** **a)** absent-minded **b)** kind **c)** cruel **d)** talented

_____ 46. **intentional** **a)** misguided **b)** accidental **c)** on purpose **d)** against the law

_____ 47. **interference** **a)** getting in the way **b)** loss of heat **c)** sudden quiet **d)** acceptance

_____ 48. **obnoxious** **a)** well-meaning **b)** unclear **c)** comical **d)** unpleasant

_____ 49. **unstable** **a)** usual **b)** unsteady **c)** strong **d)** complete

_____ 50. **utilize** **a)** suggest **b)** accept as fact **c)** control by force **d)** make use of

SCORE: (Number correct) _____ × 2 = _____ %

Unit 2: *Pretest*

In the space provided, write the letter of the choice that is closest in meaning to the **boldfaced** word.

_____ 1. **advise**   **a)** suggest   **b)** insist   **c)** plead   **d)** punish

_____ 2. **current**   **a)** modern   **b)** few in number   **c)** good tasting   **d)** likable

_____ 3. **deprive**   **a)** provide   **b)** take away   **c)** obey   **d)** copy

_____ 4. **hesitate**   **a)** hurry   **b)** forbid   **c)** consider   **d)** pause

_____ 5. **maintain**   **a)** release from captivity   **b)** keep in existence   **c)** prove to be correct   **d)** admire

_____ 6. **minimum**   **a)** largest possible   **b)** desirable   **c)** smallest possible   **d)** more than expected

_____ 7. **objection**   **a)** recommendation   **b)** dislike   **c)** reason   **d)** prize

_____ 8. **originate**   **a)** imitate   **b)** begin   **c)** impress   **d)** pretend

_____ 9. **penalize**   **a)** punish   **b)** reward   **c)** publish   **d)** give up

_____ 10. **reliable**   **a)** untrustworthy   **b)** easily tricked   **c)** dependable   **d)** unstable

_____ 11. **abrupt**   **a)** sudden   **b)** expected   **c)** delayed   **d)** loud

_____ 12. **astonish**   **a)** continue   **b)** surprise   **c)** give away   **d)** stop

_____ 13. **classify**   **a)** make clear   **b)** put up with   **c)** set aside for later   **d)** arrange by type

_____ 14. **complex**   **a)** helpful   **b)** hard to understand   **c)** comfortable   **d)** smallest possible

_____ 15. **consent**   **a)** agree to   **b)** sit down   **c)** listen   **d)** reward

_____ 16. **eager**   **a)** unforgiving   **b)** best   **c)** happily excited   **d)** good-looking

_____ 17. **endure**   **a)** punish   **b)** demand   **c)** put up with   **d)** confuse

_____ 18. **exclaim**   **a)** tell   **b)** call out   **c)** show   **d)** make clear

_____ 19. **horizontal**   **a)** careless   **b)** up and down   **c)** unexpected   **d)** extending from side to side

_____ 20. **recollect**   **a)** remember   **b)** put away   **c)** agree with   **d)** put into groups

_____ 21. **adequate**   **a)** good enough   **b)** lacking   **c)** important   **d)** not needed

_____ 22. **appeal**   **a)** request   **b)** give up   **c)** take away the outer part   **d)** repeat

_____ 23. **awkward**   **a)** charming   **b)** hostile   **c)** clumsy   **d)** easily fooled

_____ 24. **customary**   **a)** commonly done   **b)** foreign   **c)** available for sale   **d)** without value

_____ 25. **establish**   **a)** start   **b)** knock down   **c)** flatten   **d)** say again

(Continues on next page)

_____ 26. **potential**   **a)** ancestors   **b)** income   **c)** possibility   **d)** preference

_____ 27. **respond**   **a)** treat with respect   **b)** mock; treat with scorn   **c)** answer
                            d) withhold information

_____ 28. **vanish**   **a)** make shiny   **b)** disappear   **c)** make new or youthful   **d)** request

_____ 29. **variety**   **a)** opinion   **b)** assortment   **c)** reason   **d)** delay

_____ 30. **wholesome**   **a)** healthful   **b)** disgusting   **c)** hard to get   **d)** childlike

_____ 31. **brutal**   **a)** generous   **b)** brave   **c)** sympathetic   **d)** cruel

_____ 32. **discipline**   **a)** train   **b)** learn   **c)** avoid   **d)** misunderstand

_____ 33. **eliminate**   **a)** add to   **b)** get rid of   **c)** make more difficult   **d)** inform

_____ 34. **emphasis**   **a)** refusal to speak   **b)** betrayal   **c)** importance   **d)** stubborn act

_____ 35. **furthermore**   **a)** without   **b)** at a later point in time   **c)** in addition   **d)** in spite of

_____ 36. **interpret**   **a)** confuse   **b)** make an effort   **c)** light from within   **d)** explain

_____ 37. **propose**   **a)** persuade   **b)** suggest   **c)** exaggerate   **d)** point out

_____ 38. **resort**   **a)** turn (to) for help   **b)** say no to   **c)** hold a grudge   **d)** enable

_____ 39. **ultimate**   **a)** least important   **b)** inefficient   **c)** dangerous   **d)** greatest

_____ 40. **vague**   **a)** unclear   **b)** shining   **c)** in fashion   **d)** embarrassing

_____ 41. **accustomed**   **a)** unused to   **b)** in the habit of   **c)** unable to   **d)** angry at

_____ 42. **anticipate**   **a)** expect   **b)** fear   **c)** dislike   **d)** happen later

_____ 43. **linger**   **a)** hurry away   **b)** get rid of (something)   **c)** change   **d)** remain

_____ 44. **miserable**   **a)** dampened   **b)** youthful   **c)** unhappy   **d)** excited

_____ 45. **misinterpret**   **a)** have respect   **b)** prefer   **c)** understand incorrectly   **d)** get rid of

_____ 46. **occur**   **a)** disappear   **b)** repeat   **c)** respond   **d)** happen

_____ 47. **reluctant**   **a)** unwilling   **b)** eager   **c)** quick-moving   **d)** amused

_____ 48. **revise**   **a)** correct and improve   **b)** discard   **c)** copy without giving credit
                            d) fail to complete

_____ 49. **specific**   **a)** ready   **b)** unpleasantly loud   **c)** exact   **d)** willing

_____ 50. **version**   **a)** report based on one point of view   **b)** story reflecting many opinions
                            c) inaccurate account   **d)** deliberately malicious story

---

SCORE: (Number correct) _____ × 2 = _____ %

Unit 2: *Posttest*

In the space provided, write the letter of the choice that is closest in meaning to the **boldfaced** word.

____ 1. **adequate**   **a)** good enough **b)** lacking **c)** important **d)** not needed

____ 2. **appeal**   **a)** request **b)** say no to **c)** take away the outer part **d)** repeat

____ 3. **awkward**   **a)** charming **b)** hostile **c)** clumsy **d)** easily fooled

____ 4. **customary**   **a)** commonly done **b)** foreign **c)** available for sale **d)** without value

____ 5. **establish**   **a)** say again **b)** knock down **c)** flatten **d)** start

____ 6. **eager**   **a)** unforgiving **b)** best **c)** happily excited **d)** good-looking

____ 7. **endure**   **a)** punish **b)** demand **c)** put up with **d)** confuse

____ 8. **exclaim**   **a)** tell **b)** call out **c)** show **d)** make clear

____ 9. **horizontal**   **a)** careless **b)** up and down **c)** unexpected **d)** extending from side to side

____ 10. **recollect**   **a)** remember **b)** put away **c)** agree with **d)** put into groups

____ 11. **abrupt**   **a)** sudden **b)** expected **c)** delayed **d)** loud

____ 12. **astonish**   **a)** continue **b)** surprise **c)** give away **d)** stop

____ 13. **classify**   **a)** make clear **b)** put up with **c)** set aside for later **d)** arrange by type

____ 14. **complex**   **a)** helpful **b)** hard to understand **c)** comfortable **d)** smallest possible

____ 15. **consent**   **a)** agree to **b)** sit down **c)** listen **d)** reward

____ 16. **minimum**   **a)** largest possible **b)** desirable **c)** smallest possible **d)** more than expected

____ 17. **objection**   **a)** recommendation **b)** dislike **c)** reason **d)** prize

____ 18. **originate**   **a)** imitate **b)** begin **c)** impress **d)** pretend

____ 19. **penalize**   **a)** punish **b)** reward **c)** publish **d)** give up

____ 20. **reliable**   **a)** untrustworthy **b)** easily tricked **c)** dependable **d)** unstable

____ 21. **advise**   **a)** suggest **b)** insist **c)** plead **d)** punish

____ 22. **current**   **a)** modern **b)** few in number **c)** good tasting **d)** likable

____ 23. **deprive**   **a)** provide **b)** take away **c)** obey **d)** copy

____ 24. **hesitate**   **a)** hurry **b)** forbid **c)** consider **d)** pause

____ 25. **maintain**   **a)** release from captivity **b)** keep in existence **c)** prove to be correct **d)** admire

(Continues on next page)

_____ 26. **brutal** **a)** cruel **b)** brave **c)** sympathetic **d)** generous

_____ 27. **discipline** **a)** avoid **b)** learn **c)** train **d)** misunderstand

_____ 28. **eliminate** **a)** add to **b)** make more difficult **c)** get rid of **d)** inform

_____ 29. **emphasis** **a)** importance **b)** betrayal **c)** refusal to speak **d)** stubborn act

_____ 30. **furthermore** **a)** without **b)** at a later point in time **c)** in spite of **d)** in addition

_____ 31. **occur** **a)** disappear **b)** happen **c)** respond **d)** repeat

_____ 32. **reluctant** **a)** quick-moving **b)** eager **c)** unwilling **d)** amused

_____ 33. **revise** **a)** copy without giving credit **b)** discard **c)** correct and improve
     d) fail to complete

_____ 34. **specific** **a)** ready **b)** exact **c)** unpleasantly loud **d)** willing

_____ 35. **version** **a)** deliberately malicious story **b)** story reflecting many opinions
     c) inaccurate account **d)** report based on one point of view

_____ 36. **potential** **a)** ancestors **b)** possibility **c)** income **d)** preference

_____ 37. **respond** **a)** treat with respect **b)** mock; treat with scorn **c)** withhold information
     d) answer

_____ 38. **vanish** **a)** disappear **b)** make shiny **c)** make new or youthful **d)** request

_____ 39. **variety** **a)** opinion **b)** delay **c)** reason **d)** assortment

_____ 40. **wholesome** **a)** disgusting **b)** healthful **c)** hard to get **d)** childlike

_____ 41. **accustomed** **a)** unused to **b)** unable to **c)** in the habit of **d)** angry at

_____ 42. **anticipate** **a)** happen later **b)** fear **c)** dislike **d)** expect

_____ 43. **linger** **a)** hurry away **b)** get rid of (something) **c)** remain **d)** change

_____ 44. **miserable** **a)** dampened **b)** unhappy **c)** youthful **d)** excited

_____ 45. **misinterpret** **a)** understand incorrectly **b)** prefer **c)** have respect **d)** get rid of

_____ 46. **interpret** **a)** confuse **b)** explain **c)** light from within **d)** make an effort

_____ 47. **propose** **a)** persuade **b)** point out **c)** exaggerate **d)** suggest

_____ 48. **resort** **a)** say no to **b)** enable **c)** hold a grudge **d)** turn (to) for help

_____ 49. **ultimate** **a)** least important **b)** greatest **c)** dangerous **d)** inefficient

_____ 50. **vague** **a)** shining **b)** unclear **c)** in fashion **d)** embarrassing

SCORE: (Number correct) _____ × 2 = _____ %

Unit 3: *Pretest*

In the space provided, write the letter of the choice that is closest in meaning to the **boldfaced** word.

____ 1. **assume**
a) suppose to be true   **b)** prove to be false
c) hold no opinion about (something)   **d)** argue hotly

____ 2. **conscious**   **a)** drowsy   **b)** awake   **c)** depressed   **d)** purposeful

____ 3. **exhaust**   **a)** refill   **b)** remove from sight   **c)** use up   **d)** fall

____ 4. **external**   **a)** buried deeply   **b)** outer   **c)** unimportant   **d)** common

____ 5. **incredible**   **a)** unbelievable   **b)** showy   **c)** humble   **d)** wasteful

____ 6. **internal**   **a)** inner   **b)** uncommon   **c)** easy   **d)** understood by few

____ 7. **maximum**   **a)** not popular   **b)** greatest in amount   **c)** worst   **d)** comfortable

____ 8. **objective**   **a)** bad influence   **b)** reason to believe   **c)** insult   **d)** goal

____ 9. **protest**   **a)** speak out against   **b)** encourage   **c)** prove   **d)** debate

____ 10. **remedy**
a) source of amusement   **b)** usual manner of doing something
c) collection of writings   **d)** cure

____ 11. **artificial**   **a)** natural   **b)** impressive   **c)** not natural   **d)** worn out

____ 12. **complicate**   **a)** smooth over   **b)** adjust   **c)** make difficult   **d)** divide

____ 13. **conscience**
a) sense of being awake   **b)** inability to decide
c) sense of right and wrong   **d)** skill with numbers

____ 14. **counsel**   **a)** improve   **b)** approve   **c)** give advice   **d)** revise

____ 15. **detect**   **a)** obtain   **b)** complain   **c)** remark   **d)** notice

____ 16. **frequency**
a) how often something happens   **b)** rate of speed   **c)** volume of sound
d) source of sound

____ 17. **represent**
a) avoid talking about   **b)** prefer over another choice   **c)** be a symbol for
d) allow to happen

____ 18. **temporary**
a) expected to last forever   **b)** impossible to achieve
c) serving for a limited time   **d)** clearly seen

____ 19. **transparent**   **a)** solid   **b)** dark in color   **c)** seen through easily   **d)** unusual

____ 20. **triumph**   **a)** victory   **b)** defeat   **c)** compromise   **d)** battle

____ 21. **detract**   **a)** take away   **b)** grow   **c)** speed up   **d)** pass by

____ 22. **foresight**   **a)** purpose   **b)** understanding   **c)** cure   **d)** careful planning

____ 23. **intense**   **a)** unreal   **b)** frightened   **c)** unkind   **d)** strong

____ 24. **interval**   **a)** word group   **b)** time in between   **c)** system   **d)** victory

____ 25. **prosper**   **a)** do poorly   **b)** become old   **c)** succeed   **d)** help

(Continues on next page)

_____ 26. **strive**   **a)** do well   **b)** take away   **c)** feel good   **d)** try hard

_____ 27. **substance**   **a)** care   **b)** knowledge   **c)** material   **d)** hard work

_____ 28. **tolerance**   **a)** acceptance   **b)** avoidance   **c)** experience   **d)** confusion

_____ 29. **trait**   **a)** story   **b)** feature   **c)** unexpected gift   **d)** journey

_____ 30. **withdraw**   **a)** write down   **b)** take back   **c)** make shorter   **d)** make happy

_____ 31. **approximately** **a)** never   **b)** under   **c)** almost   **d)** more than

_____ 32. **consistent**   **a)** made up of   **b)** regular   **c)** useful   **d)** important

_____ 33. **cope**   **a)** measure   **b)** look at   **c)** deal with   **d)** give up

_____ 34. **evaluate**   **a)** ignore   **b)** use up   **c)** judge   **d)** take away

_____ 35. **observe**   **a)** watch closely   **b)** disturb   **c)** bring together   **d)** control

_____ 36. **phrase**   **a)** period of time   **b)** group of words   **c)** highest point   **d)** outer layer

_____ 37. **practical**   **a)** useful   **b)** expensive   **c)** silly   **d)** unplanned

_____ 38. **random**   **a)** rare   **b)** common   **c)** expensive   **d)** unplanned

_____ 39. **significant**   **a)** lucky   **b)** available   **c)** important   **d)** busy

_____ 40. **sole**   **a)** delayed   **b)** deep   **c)** early   **d)** only

_____ 41. **authentic**   **a)** real   **b)** old   **c)** expensive   **d)** useful

_____ 42. **characteristic** **a)** unexpected   **b)** usual   **c)** modern   **d)** weird

_____ 43. **concept**   **a)** period of time   **b)** goal   **c)** memory   **d)** idea

_____ 44. **confront**   **a)** succeed   **b)** interrupt   **c)** face   **d)** ignore

_____ 45. **disrupt**   **a)** watch closely   **b)** describe   **c)** upset   **d)** complain

_____ 46. **eligible**   **a)** qualified   **b)** far away   **c)** able to be read   **d)** worthless

_____ 47. **harsh**   **a)** new   **b)** loud   **c)** fair   **d)** cruel

_____ 48. **remote**   **a)** low   **b)** far away   **c)** unusual   **d)** able to be moved

_____ 49. **shallow**   **a)** friendly   **b)** solid   **c)** not deep   **d)** not strong

_____ 50. **thrive**   **a)** raise up   **b)** do well   **c)** grow weak   **d)** need extra care

---

SCORE: (Number correct) _____ × 2 = _____ %

Unit 3: *Posttest*

In the space provided, write the letter of the choice that is closest in meaning to the **boldfaced** word.

_____ 1. **detract**   a) speed up   b) grow   c) take away   d) pass by

_____ 2. **foresight**   a) purpose   b) understanding   c) cure   d) careful planning

_____ 3. **intense**   a) strong   b) frightened   c) unkind   d) unreal

_____ 4. **interval**   a) word group   b) system   c) time in between   d) victory

_____ 5. **prosper**   a) do poorly   b) become old   c) succeed   d) help

_____ 6. **internal**   a) uncommon   b) inner   c) easy   d) understood by few

_____ 7. **maximum**   a) not popular   b) comfortable   c) worst   d) greatest in amount

_____ 8. **objective**   a) bad influence   b) reason to believe   c) goal   d) insult

_____ 9. **protest**   a) encourage   b) speak out against   c) prove   d) debate

_____ 10. **remedy**   a) cure   b) source of amusement   c) usual manner of doing something
        d) collection of writings

_____ 11. **assume**   a) hold no opinion about (something)   b) prove to be false
        c) suppose to be true   d) argue hotly

_____ 12. **conscious**   a) awake   b) drowsy   c) depressed   d) purposeful

_____ 13. **exhaust**   a) use up   b) remove from sight   c) refill   d) fall

_____ 14. **external**   a) buried deeply   b) unimportant   c) outer   d) common

_____ 15. **incredible**   a) wasteful   b) showy   c) humble   d) unbelievable

_____ 16. **frequency**   a) volume of sound   b) rate of speed   c) how often something happens
        d) source of sound

_____ 17. **represent**   a) be a symbol for   b) prefer over another choice   c) avoid talking about
        d) allow to happen

_____ 18. **temporary**   a) expected to last forever   b) serving for a limited time
        c) impossible to achieve   d) clearly seen

_____ 19. **transparent**   a) solid   b) dark in color   c) unusual   d) seen through easily

_____ 20. **triumph**   a) compromise   b) defeat   c) victory   d) battle

_____ 21. **artificial**   a) natural   b) not natural   c) impressive   d) worn out

_____ 22. **complicate**   a) make difficult   b) adjust   c) smooth over   d) divide

_____ 23. **conscience**   a) sense of right and wrong   b) inability to decide
        c) sense of being awake   d) skill with numbers

_____ 24. **counsel**   a) improve   b) give advice   c) approve   d) revise

_____ 25. **detect**   a) obtain   b) complain   c) notice   d) remark

(Continues on next page)

_____ 26. **eligible** a) far away b) qualified c) able to be read d) worthless

_____ 27. **harsh** a) new b) loud c) cruel d) fair

_____ 28. **remote** a) far away b) low c) unusual d) able to be moved

_____ 29. **shallow** a) friendly b) solid c) not strong d) not deep

_____ 30. **thrive** a) do well b) raise up c) grow weak d) need extra care

_____ 31. **authentic** a) expensive b) old c) real d) useful

_____ 32. **characteristic** a) usual b) unexpected c) modern d) weird

_____ 33. **concept** a) period of time b) goal c) idea d) memory

_____ 34. **confront** a) succeed b) face c) interrupt d) ignore

_____ 35. **disrupt** a) watch closely b) describe c) complain d) upset

_____ 36. **phrase** a) group of words b) period of time c) highest point d) outer layer

_____ 37. **practical** a) expensive b) useful c) silly d) unplanned

_____ 38. **random** a) rare b) common c) unplanned d) expensive

_____ 39. **significant** a) lucky b) available c) busy d) important

_____ 40. **sole** a) delayed b) deep c) only d) early

_____ 41. **approximately** a) never b) almost c) under d) more than

_____ 42. **consistent** a) regular b) made up of c) useful d) important

_____ 43. **cope** a) measure b) look at c) give up d) deal with

_____ 44. **evaluate** a) ignore b) use up c) take away d) judge

_____ 45. **observe** a) disturb b) watch closely c) bring together d) control

_____ 46. **strive** a) do well b) try hard c) feel good d) take away

_____ 47. **substance** a) material b) knowledge c) care d) hard work

_____ 48. **tolerance** a) experience b) avoidance c) acceptance d) confusion

_____ 49. **trait** a) feature b) story c) unexpected gift d) journey

_____ 50. **withdraw** a) write down b) make happy c) make shorter d) take back

---

SCORE: (Number correct) _____ × 2 = _____ %

Name: _____

Unit 4: *Pretest*

In the space provided, write the letter of the choice that is closest in meaning to the **boldfaced** word.

_____ 1. **apparent** a) impossible to see with the naked eye b) made up of many small parts
c) obvious d) hard to understand

_____ 2. **automatic** a) easily moved b) operating by itself c) unable to change
d) improving over time

_____ 3. **burden** a) hardship b) joy c) reply d) payment

_____ 4. **economical** a) wasteful b) intelligent c) thrifty d) forgiving

_____ 5. **extravagant** a) critical b) wasteful c) wise d) messy

_____ 6. **fulfill** a) carry out b) fail at a task c) understand another's feelings d) give advice

_____ 7. **influence** a) misunderstand b) excuse c) be offended d) persuade

_____ 8. **security** a) protection b) loneliness c) immaturity d) ridicule

_____ 9. **sympathize** a) share feeling b) object c) refuse d) cooperate

_____ 10. **transfer** a) find fault b) discontinue c) send from a place d) inspect

_____ 11. **appropriate** a) rude b) impulsive c) unwise d) proper

_____ 12. **bewilder** a) calm b) confuse c) accept d) explain

_____ 13. **communicate** a) anger b) inform c) hurry d) mistake

_____ 14. **deceive** a) mislead b) encourage c) prevent d) forbid

_____ 15. **earnest** a) dishonest b) wealthy c) pleasant d) sincere

_____ 16. **emotion** a) feeling b) eyesight c) movement d) payment

_____ 17. **fiction** a) made up b) exciting c) violent d) romantic

_____ 18. **investigate** a) abandon b) make secure c) examine d) insist

_____ 19. **legible** a) heavy b) clear c) empty d) noisy

_____ 20. **theory** a) opportunity b) guess c) certainty d) excuse

_____ 21. **assure** a) argue with b) remind c) agree with d) promise

_____ 22. **crucial** a) useless b) ugly c) important d) famous

_____ 23. **distract** a) make sad b) support c) cause to disappear d) cause to turn away

_____ 24. **extraordinary** a) left over b) unusual c) normal d) very simple

_____ 25. **hostile** a) unfriendly b) frightened c) important d) growing

(Continues on next page)

____ 26. **humiliate**   **a)** misunderstand   **b)** embarrass   **c)** defeat   **d)** excite

____ 27. **impulse**   **a)** sudden desire   **b)** lack of movement   **c)** difficulty   **d)** heartbeat

____ 28. **perceive**   **a)** strain   **b)** notice   **c)** lie to   **d)** prepare

____ 29. **revive**   **a)** leave alone   **b)** say again   **c)** bring back to life   **d)** embarrass

____ 30. **timid**   **a)** athletic   **b)** full of energy   **c)** careless   **d)** shy

____ 31. **abandon**   **a)** stop doing   **b)** hold onto   **c)** bring together   **d)** begin

____ 32. **alert**   **a)** bad-smelling   **b)** lazy   **c)** strong   **d)** fully awake

____ 33. **circumstances**   **a)** feelings   **b)** facts   **c)** circles   **d)** desires

____ 34. **devote**   **a)** take away   **b)** look over   **c)** give oneself   **d)** show a preference

____ 35. **dominate**   **a)** be a part of   **b)** be a leader in   **c)** drop out of   **d)** lose interest in

____ 36. **function**   **a)** purpose   **b)** topic   **c)** fact   **d)** part

____ 37. **idle**   **a)** frightened   **b)** full of energy   **c)** lonely   **d)** not active

____ 38. **overcome**   **a)** be a winner over   **b)** leave behind   **c)** see clearly   **d)** lose to

____ 39. **primary**   **a)** easy   **b)** unimportant   **c)** entertaining   **d)** main

____ 40. **theme**   **a)** main idea   **b)** difficulty   **c)** direction   **d)** river

____ 41. **disregard**   **a)** look at   **b)** get in the way of   **c)** admire   **d)** ignore

____ 42. **excerpt**   **a)** part   **b)** prize   **c)** sudden decision   **d)** trip

____ 43. **exclude**   **a)** invite   **b)** bring into   **c)** keep out   **d)** tire out

____ 44. **hinder**   **a)** find out   **b)** interfere with   **c)** bring into   **d)** put behind

____ 45. **misleading**   **a)** serious   **b)** straight   **c)** giving the wrong idea   **d)** staying close to

____ 46. **monotonous**   **a)** loud   **b)** dull   **c)** pleasant   **d)** messy

____ 47. **obtain**   **a)** get   **b)** protect   **c)** spoil   **d)** move

____ 48. **prey**   **a)** victim   **b)** leader   **c)** struggle   **d)** prayer

____ 49. **seize**   **a)** tell   **b)** stare   **c)** strain   **d)** grab

____ 50. **severe**   **a)** boring   **b)** new   **c)** serious   **d)** exciting

---

SCORE: (Number correct) _____ × 2 = _____ %

Unit 4: *Posttest*

In the space provided, write the letter of the choice that is closest in meaning to the **boldfaced** word.

_____ 1. **appropriate** a) rude b) impulsive c) proper d) unwise

_____ 2. **bewilder** a) confuse b) calm c) accept d) explain

_____ 3. **communicate** a) anger b) hurry c) inform d) mistake

_____ 4. **deceive** a) forbid b) encourage c) prevent d) mislead

_____ 5. **earnest** a) dishonest b) wealthy c) sincere d) pleasant

_____ 6. **fulfill** a) fail at a task b) carry out c) understand another's feelings d) give advice

_____ 7. **influence** a) misunderstand b) excuse c) persuade d) be offended

_____ 8. **security** a) loneliness b) protection c) immaturity d) ridicule

_____ 9. **sympathize** a) refuse b) object c) share feeling d) cooperate

_____ 10. **transfer** a) find fault b) discontinue c) inspect d) send from a place

_____ 11. **apparent** a) impossible to see with the naked eye b) made up of many small parts
c) hard to understand d) obvious

_____ 12. **automatic** a) operating by itself b) easily moved c) unable to change
d) improving over time

_____ 13. **burden** a) reply b) joy c) hardship d) payment

_____ 14. **economical** a) wasteful b) intelligent c) forgiving d) thrifty

_____ 15. **extravagant** a) critical b) wise c) wasteful d) messy

_____ 16. **assure** a) argue with b) remind c) promise d) agree with

_____ 17. **crucial** a) useless b) important c) ugly d) famous

_____ 18. **distract** a) cause to turn away b) support c) cause to disappear d) make sad

_____ 19. **extraordinary** a) left over b) normal c) unusual d) very simple

_____ 20. **hostile** a) frightened b) unfriendly c) important d) growing

_____ 21. **emotion** a) movement b) eyesight c) feeling d) payment

_____ 22. **fiction** a) romantic b) exciting c) violent d) made up

_____ 23. **investigate** a) abandon b) examine c) make secure d) insist

_____ 24. **legible** a) clear b) heavy c) empty d) noisy

_____ 25. **theory** a) opportunity b) excuse c) certainty d) guess

(Continues on next page)

103

_____ 26. **abandon** **a)** bring together **b)** hold onto **c)** stop doing **d)** begin

_____ 27. **alert** **a)** bad-smelling **b)** fully awake **c)** strong **d)** lazy

_____ 28. **circumstances** **a)** facts **b)** feelings **c)** circles **d)** desires

_____ 29. **devote** **a)** take away **b)** look over **c)** show a preference **d)** give oneself

_____ 30. **dominate** **a)** be a leader in **b)** be a part of **c)** drop out of **d)** lose interest in

_____ 31. **humiliate** **a)** misunderstand **b)** defeat **c)** embarrass **d)** excite

_____ 32. **impulse** **a)** heartbeat **b)** lack of movement **c)** difficulty **d)** sudden desire

_____ 33. **perceive** **a)** notice **b)** strain **c)** lie to **d)** prepare

_____ 34. **revive** **a)** leave alone **b)** bring back to life **c)** say again **d)** embarrass

_____ 35. **timid** **a)** shy **b)** full of energy **c)** careless **d)** athletic

_____ 36. **disregard** **a)** look at **b)** ignore **c)** admire **d)** get in the way of

_____ 37. **excerpt** **a)** trip **b)** prize **c)** sudden decision **d)** part

_____ 38. **exclude** **a)** invite **b)** keep out **c)** bring into **d)** tire out

_____ 39. **hinder** **a)** interfere with **b)** find out **c)** bring into **d)** put behind

_____ 40. **misleading** **a)** serious **b)** giving the wrong idea **c)** straight **d)** staying close to

_____ 41. **function** **a)** topic **b)** purpose **c)** fact **d)** part

_____ 42. **idle** **a)** frightened **b)** full of energy **c)** not active **d)** lonely

_____ 43. **overcome** **a)** leave behind **b)** be a winner over **c)** see clearly **d)** lose to

_____ 44. **primary** **a)** easy **b)** unimportant **c)** main **d)** entertaining

_____ 45. **theme** **a)** difficulty **b)** main idea **c)** direction **d)** river

_____ 46. **monotonous** **a)** loud **b)** pleasant **c)** dull **d)** messy

_____ 47. **obtain** **a)** protect **b)** get **c)** spoil **d)** move

_____ 48. **prey** **a)** prayer **b)** leader **c)** struggle **d)** victim

_____ 49. **seize** **a)** tell **b)** stare **c)** grab **d)** strain

_____ 50. **severe** **a)** serious **b)** new **c)** boring **d)** exciting

---

SCORE: (Number correct) _____ × 2 = _____ %

Name: _____

Unit 5: *Pretest*

In the space provided, write the letter of the choice that is closest in meaning to the **boldfaced** word.

_____ 1. **conflict** a) period of time b) point of view c) lesson d) disagreement

_____ 2. **possess** a) run after b) adjust c) leave unchanged d) own

_____ 3. **procedure** a) method b) opinion c) public d) piece of property

_____ 4. **renew** a) create b) make active again c) force one's will upon d) attempt

_____ 5. **resources** a) supplies b) inventions c) responses d) agreements

_____ 6. **stress** a) tension b) relaxation c) enjoyment d) excitement

_____ 7. **sufficient** a) less than is needed b) humorous c) empty d) enough

_____ 8. **unanimous** a) poorly thought out b) one-sided c) based on complete agreement
d) mistaken

_____ 9. **vary** a) change b) insist c) remain the same d) reduce in size

_____ 10. **vicinity** a) heated argument b) area around a place c) written pamphlet
d) type of lamp

_____ 11. **abolish** a) make smooth b) argue c) get rid of d) pay for

_____ 12. **corrupt** a) sudden b) not honest c) careful d) not friendly

_____ 13. **decay** a) break down b) make a decision c) rebuild d) make clear

_____ 14. **expand** a) spend b) shrink c) punish d) grow

_____ 15. **flexible** a) able to speak b) able to slow down c) able to bend d) able to walk

_____ 16. **nevertheless** a) because b) afterward c) always d) even so

_____ 17. **precise** a) exact b) busy c) large d) neglectful

_____ 18. **reform** a) annoy b) make clear c) make better d) confuse

_____ 19. **tendency** a) group of ten b) leaning toward c) working hard d) setting a limit

_____ 20. **vast** a) well known b) silly c) very large d) frightening

_____ 21. **assert** a) state as true b) tell a lie c) put limits on d) get ready for

_____ 22. **clarify** a) doubt b) explain c) create d) stop

_____ 23. **evade** a) make small b) break down c) get away from d) make longer

_____ 24. **extend** a) make longer b) make up c) make ready d) make small

_____ 25. **negligent** a) watchful b) tired c) not bending d) careless

(Continues on next page)

_____ 26. **precaution**   a) cure   b) problem   c) something done to fix a problem
d) something done beforehand

_____ 27. **preconception**   a) judgment made in advance   b) decision   c) problem   d) area nearby

_____ 28. **resemble**   a) see again   b) look like   c) worry about   d) be angry with

_____ 29. **rigid**   a) like new   b) not bending   c) not friendly   d) hard to see

_____ 30. **vertical**   a) side to side   b) up and down   c) all around   d) truthful

_____ 31. **anxious**   a) sleepy   b) sick   c) busy   d) worried

_____ 32. **comprehend**   a) scorn   b) repeat   c) protect   d) understand

_____ 33. **convince**   a) cause to believe   b) refuse to accept   c) disregard   d) clean up

_____ 34. **dramatic**   a) impressive   b) hard to notice   c) odd   d) boring

_____ 35. **frank**   a) untruthful   b) youthful   c) honest   d) painful

_____ 36. **illustrate**   a) give an example   b) destroy   c) repair   d) send off

_____ 37. **impression**   a) lie   b) pattern   c) opinion   d) center (of something)

_____ 38. **inferior**   a) highly valued   b) poor in quality   c) less expensive
d) unbreakable

_____ 39. **overwhelm**   a) dissolve   b) understand   c) make helpless   d) make whole

_____ 40. **thorough**   a) carefully done   b) wasted   c) forgotten   d) well-paying

_____ 41. **acquire**   a) appreciate   b) go before   c) need   d) get

_____ 42. **commitment**   a) promise   b) symbol   c) talk   d) group of people

_____ 43. **formal**   a) proper   b) previous   c) later   d) complete

_____ 44. **fragment**   a) injury   b) copy   c) true statement   d) small part

_____ 45. **fundamental**   a) basic   b) broken   c) enjoyable   d) thoughtful

_____ 46. **precede**   a) come after   b) interrupt   c) be a part of   d) go before

_____ 47. **resent**   a) stand for   b) feel angry at   c) give away   d) make up with

_____ 48. **solemn**   a) lazy   b) basic   c) serious   d) quiet

_____ 49. **spite**   a) desire to hurt   b) desire to please   c) long speech   d) sense of humor

_____ 50. **symbolize**   a) look at   b) point to   c) talk to   d) stand for

SCORE: (Number correct) _____ × 2 = _____ %

Unit 5: *Posttest*

In the space provided, write the letter of the choice that is closest in meaning to the **boldfaced** word.

_____ 1. **abolish**   a) make smooth   b) argue   c) pay for   d) get rid of

_____ 2. **corrupt**   a) not honest   b) sudden   c) careful   d) not friendly

_____ 3. **decay**   a) make a decision   b) break down   c) rebuild   d) make clear

_____ 4. **expand**   a) spend   b) shrink   c) grow   d) punish

_____ 5. **flexible**   a) able to speak   b) able to slow down   c) able to walk   d) able to bend

_____ 6. **stress**   a) enjoyment   b) relaxation   c) tension   d) excitement

_____ 7. **sufficient**   a) less than is needed   b) humorous   c) enough   d) empty

_____ 8. **unanimous**   a) based on complete agreement   b) one-sided   c) poorly thought out
d) mistaken

_____ 9. **vary**   a) insist   b) change   c) remain the same   d) reduce in size

_____ 10. **vicinity**   a) area around a place   b) heated argument   c) written pamphlet
d) type of lamp

_____ 11. **assert**   a) put limits on   b) tell a lie   c) state as true   d) get ready for

_____ 12. **clarify**   a) doubt   b) stop   c) create   d) explain

_____ 13. **evade**   a) make small   b) get away from   c) break down   d) make longer

_____ 14. **extend**   a) make ready   b) make up   c) make longer   d) make small

_____ 15. **negligent**   a) careless   b) tired   c) not bending   d) watchful

_____ 16. **nevertheless**   a) because   b) afterward   c) even so   d) always

_____ 17. **precise**   a) busy   b) exact   c) large   d) neglectful

_____ 18. **reform**   a) annoy   b) make clear   c) confuse   d) make better

_____ 19. **tendency**   a) leaning toward   b) group of ten   c) working hard   d) setting a limit

_____ 20. **vast**   a) well known   b) very large   c) silly   d) frightening

_____ 21. **conflict**   a) disagreement   b) point of view   c) lesson   d) period of time

_____ 22. **possess**   a) own   b) adjust   c) leave unchanged   d) run after

_____ 23. **procedure**   a) public   b) opinion   c) method   d) piece of property

_____ 24. **renew**   a) make active again   b) create   c) force one's will upon   d) attempt

_____ 25. **resources**   a) inventions   b) supplies   c) responses   d) agreements

(Continues on next page)

_____ 26. **illustrate** **a)** send off **b)** destroy **c)** repair **d)** give an example

_____ 27. **impression** **a)** lie **b)** opinion **c)** pattern **d)** center (of something)

_____ 28. **inferior** **a)** poor in quality **b)** unbreakable **c)** less expensive
d) highly valued

_____ 29. **overwhelm** **a)** dissolve **b)** understand **c)** make whole **d)** make helpless

_____ 30. **thorough** **a)** forgotten **b)** wasted **c)** carefully done **d)** well-paying

_____ 31. **anxious** **a)** sleepy **b)** worried **c)** busy **d)** sick

_____ 32. **comprehend** **a)** understand **b)** repeat **c)** protect **d)** scorn

_____ 33. **convince** **a)** disregard **b)** refuse to accept **c)** cause to believe **d)** clean up

_____ 34. **dramatic** **a)** boring **b)** hard to notice **c)** odd **d)** impressive

_____ 35. **frank** **a)** untruthful **b)** honest **c)** youthful **d)** painful

_____ 36. **acquire** **a)** appreciate **b)** get **c)** need **d)** go before

_____ 37. **commitment** **a)** group of people **b)** symbol **c)** talk **d)** promise

_____ 38. **formal** **a)** previous **b)** proper **c)** later **d)** complete

_____ 39. **fragment** **a)** small part **b)** copy **c)** true statement **d)** injury

_____ 40. **fundamental** **a)** enjoyable **b)** broken **c)** basic **d)** thoughtful

_____ 41. **precede** **a)** be a part of **b)** interrupt **c)** come after **d)** go before

_____ 42. **resent** **a)** stand for **b)** give away **c)** feel angry at **d)** make up with

_____ 43. **solemn** **a)** serious **b)** basic **c)** lazy **d)** quiet

_____ 44. **spite** **a)** long speech **b)** desire to please **c)** desire to hurt **d)** sense of humor

_____ 45. **symbolize** **a)** stand for **b)** point to **c)** talk to **d)** look at

_____ 46. **precaution** **a)** cure **b)** problem **c)** something done to fix a problem
d) something done beforehand

_____ 47. **preconception** **a)** area nearby **b)** decision **c)** problem **d)** judgment made in advance

_____ 48. **resemble** **a)** see again **b)** worry about **c)** look like **d)** be angry with

_____ 49. **rigid** **a)** not bending **b)** like new **c)** not friendly **d)** hard to see

_____ 50. **vertical** **a)** side to side **b)** all around **c)** up and down **d)** truthful

SCORE: (Number correct) _____ × 2 = _____ %

Pretest / Posttest

NAME: _____

SECTION: _____ DATE: _____

SCORE: _____

ANSWER SHEET

1. ____	26. ____	51. ____	76. ____
2. ____	27. ____	52. ____	77. ____
3. ____	28. ____	53. ____	78. ____
4. ____	29. ____	54. ____	79. ____
5. ____	30. ____	55. ____	80. ____
6. ____	31. ____	56. ____	81. ____
7. ____	32. ____	57. ____	82. ____
8. ____	33. ____	58. ____	83. ____
9. ____	34. ____	59. ____	84. ____
10. ____	35. ____	60. ____	85. ____
11. ____	36. ____	61. ____	86. ____
12. ____	37. ____	62. ____	87. ____
13. ____	38. ____	63. ____	88. ____
14. ____	39. ____	64. ____	89. ____
15. ____	40. ____	65. ____	90. ____
16. ____	41. ____	66. ____	91. ____
17. ____	42. ____	67. ____	92. ____
18. ____	43. ____	68. ____	93. ____
19. ____	44. ____	69. ____	94. ____
20. ____	45. ____	70. ____	95. ____
21. ____	46. ____	71. ____	96. ____
22. ____	47. ____	72. ____	97. ____
23. ____	48. ____	73. ____	98. ____
24. ____	49. ____	74. ____	99. ____
25. ____	50. ____	75. ____	100. ____

ANSWER KEY

1. b	26. d	51. b	76. c
2. a	27. a	52. c	77. a
3. d	28. b	53. d	78. d
4. a	29. c	54. a	79. b
5. b	30. a	55. a	80. d
6. b	31. a	56. d	81. c
7. a	32. b	57. a	82. d
8. c	33. c	58. c	83. b
9. b	34. b	59. a	84. d
10. a	35. c	60. b	85. a
11. a	36. b	61. a	86. c
12. a	37. b	62. c	87. b
13. c	38. a	63. b	88. a
14. b	39. a	64. a	89. d
15. a	40. d	65. a	90. c
16. d	41. d	66. b	91. c
17. a	42. b	67. d	92. c
18. b	43. a	68. a	93. c
19. a	44. c	69. c	94. d
20. d	45. b	70. b	95. c
21. a	46. d	71. c	96. d
22. c	47. a	72. a	97. a
23. b	48. b	73. c	98. c
24. d	49. a	74. c	99. a
25. a	50. b	75. a	100. c

ANSWER KEY

1. c	26. c	51. a	76. b
2. d	27. d	52. d	77. d
3. b	28. a	53. b	78. a
4. d	29. a	54. a	79. c
5. b	30. b	55. c	80. d
6. c	31. c	56. d	81. d
7. c	32. a	57. c	82. b
8. d	33. b	58. b	83. b
9. b	34. a	59. a	84. c
10. c	35. d	60. c	85. a
11. d	36. c	61. b	86. b
12. c	37. d	62. d	87. d
13. b	38. d	63. d	88. a
14. d	39. c	64. b	89. d
15. c	40. a	65. d	90. b
16. d	41. b	66. b	91. d
17. a	42. c	67. d	92. c
18. c	43. a	68. a	93. a
19. c	44. b	69. b	94. c
20. d	45. c	70. d	95. b
21. c	46. d	71. c	96. b
22. b	47. d	72. d	97. c
23. a	48. c	73. b	98. a
24. c	49. d	74. c	99. b
25. d	50. c	75. d	100. a

Answers to the Unit Pretests and Posttests:
GROUNDWORK FOR A BETTER VOCABULARY

Unit One		Unit Two		Unit Three		Unit Four		Unit Five	
Pretest	*Posttest*	*Pretest*	*Posttest*	*Pretest*	*Posttest*	*Pretest*	*Posttest*	*Pretest*	*Posttest*
1. b	1. a	1. a	1. a	1. a	1. c	1. c	1. c	1. d	1. d
2. b	2. b	2. a	2. a	2. b	2. d	2. b	2. a	2. d	2. a
3. c	3. d	3. b	3. c	3. c	3. a	3. a	3. c	3. a	3. b
4. d	4. c	4. d	4. a	4. b	4. c	4. c	4. d	4. b	4. c
5. d	5. d	5. b	5. a	5. a	5. c	5. b	5. c	5. a	5. d
6. a	6. c	6. c	6. c	6. a	6. b	6. a	6. b	6. a	6. c
7. b	7. a	7. b	7. c	7. b	7. d	7. d	7. c	7. d	7. c
8. a	8. b	8. b	8. b	8. d	8. c	8. a	8. b	8. c	8. a
9. c	9. d	9. a	9. d	9. a	9. b	9. a	9. c	9. a	9. b
10. a	10. c	10. c	10. a	10. d	10. a	10. c	10. d	10. b	10. a
11. d	11. c	11. a	11. a	11. c	11. c	11. d	11. d	11. c	11. c
12. c	12. b	12. b	12. b	12. c	12. a	12. b	12. a	12. b	12. d
13. a	13. c	13. d	13. d	13. c	13. a	13. b	13. c	13. a	13. b
14. a	14. d	14. b	14. b	14. c	14. c	14. c	14. d	14. d	14. c
15. b	15. b	15. a	15. a	15. d	15. d	15. d	15. c	15. c	15. a
16. a	16. c	16. c	16. c	16. a	16. c	16. a	16. c	16. d	16. c
17. d	17. a	17. c	17. b	17. c	17. a	17. a	17. b	17. a	17. b
18. b	18. c	18. b	18. b	18. c	18. b	18. c	18. a	18. c	18. d
19. b	19. a	19. d	19. a	19. c	19. d	19. b	19. c	19. b	19. a
20. d	20. c	20. a	20. c	20. a	20. c	20. b	20. b	20. c	20. b
21. d	21. a	21. a	21. a	21. a	21. b	21. d	21. c	21. a	21. a
22. a	22. a	22. a	22. a	22. d	22. a	22. c	22. d	22. b	22. a
23. b	23. d	23. c	23. b	23. d	23. a	23. d	23. b	23. c	23. c
24. a	24. b	24. a	24. d	24. b	24. b	24. b	24. a	24. a	24. a
25. c	25. c	25. a	25. b	25. c	25. c	25. a	25. d	25. d	25. b
26. b	26. d	26. c	26. a	26. d	26. b	26. b	26. c	26. d	26. d
27. b	27. a	27. c	27. c	27. c	27. c	27. a	27. b	27. a	27. b
28. d	28. c	28. b	28. c	28. a	28. a	28. b	28. a	28. b	28. a
29. a	29. b	29. b	29. a	29. b	29. d	29. c	29. d	29. b	29. d
30. c	30. a	30. a	30. d	30. b	30. a	30. d	30. a	30. b	30. c
31. d	31. b	31. d	31. b	31. c	31. c	31. a	31. c	31. d	31. b
32. c	32. b	32. a	32. b	32. b	32. a	32. d	32. d	32. d	32. a
33. a	33. d	33. b	33. c	33. c	33. c	33. b	33. a	33. a	33. c
34. a	34. c	34. c	34. b	34. c	34. b	34. c	34. b	34. a	34. d
35. c	35. d	35. c	35. d	35. a	35. d	35. b	35. a	35. c	35. b
36. d	36. a	36. d	36. b	36. b	36. a	36. a	36. b	36. a	36. b
37. a	37. b	37. b	37. d	37. a	37. b	37. d	37. d	37. c	37. d
38. d	38. c	38. a	38. a	38. d	38. c	38. a	38. b	38. b	38. b
39. b	39. d	39. d	39. d	39. c	39. d	39. d	39. a	39. c	39. a
40. c	40. a	40. a	40. b	40. d	40. c	40. a	40. b	40. a	40. c
41. d	41. c	41. b	41. c	41. a	41. b	41. d	41. b	41. d	41. d
42. c	42. b	42. a	42. d	42. b	42. a	42. a	42. c	42. a	42. c
43. b	43. c	43. d	43. c	43. d	43. d	43. c	43. b	43. a	43. a
44. d	44. b	44. c	44. b	44. c	44. d	44. b	44. c	44. d	44. c
45. a	45. b	45. c	45. a	45. c	45. b	45. c	45. b	45. a	45. a
46. a	46. c	46. d	46. b	46. a	46. b	46. b	46. c	46. d	46. d
47. c	47. a	47. a	47. d	47. d	47. a	47. a	47. b	47. b	47. d
48. b	48. d	48. a	48. d	48. b	48. c	48. a	48. d	48. c	48. c
49. c	49. b	49. c	49. b	49. c	49. a	49. d	49. c	49. a	49. a
50. b	50. d	50. a	50. b	50. b	50. d	50. c	50. a	50. d	50. c

Name: _____

Mastery Test: *Chapter 1 (Johnny Appleseed; The Lovable Leech?)*

PART A. Using the answer line, complete each item below with the correct word from the box.

a. **challenge**	b. **fertile**	c. **peculiar**
d. **surplus**	e. **transform**	

_____ 1. Being polite to my rude boss is a ___.

_____ 2. Mr. and Mrs. Ring chose ___ names for their daughters—Ruby and Opal.

_____ 3. By painting on colorful designs, Carmine ___ed an old wooden chair into a work of art.

_____ 4. Our neighbor thinks he makes his houseplant soil more ___ by adding coffee grounds to it.

_____ 5. My boss at the bakery lets me take home ___ bagels at night because he bakes fresh ones every day.

PART B. Using the answer line, complete each item below with the correct word from the box.

f. **dependent**	g. **preference**	h. **principal**
i. **solitary**	j. **suitable**	

_____ 6. My boss feels that long hair on men is ___ in an office if the hair is neatly tied back.

_____ 7. There are several causes of lung cancer, but the ___ cause is cigarette smoking.

_____ 8. My boyfriend wants to get married right away, but my ___ is to live together a while.

_____ 9. Although most animals' bodies create their own vitamin C, humans are ___ upon their diet for vitamin C.

_____ 10. The weak stem of a certain wild iris can support only one flower at a time. Each morning, a ___ flower blooms and then dies at night, making room for the next morning's flower.

SCORE: (Number correct) _____ × 10 = _____ %

Mastery Test: *Chapter 2 (Finding Fault; Hobbies)*

PART A. Using the answer line, complete each item below with the correct word from the box.

a. **analyze**	b. **category**	c. **critical**
d. **deliberate**	e. **frustration**	

_____ 1. Despite its name, the firefly is in the same insect ___ as a beetle, not a fly.

_____ 2. After years of ___, the author not only finally sold a novel; he won a prize for it.

_____ 3. If you carefully ___ your monthly expenses, you'll probably find some ways to save money.

_____ 4. In a ___ effort to annoy me, my neighbor leaves his gate open so that his huge German shepherd can run after my little poodle.

_____ 5. Not wishing to be ___ of her husband's first cooking effort, Margo said, "You're very creative to think of stuffing baked potatoes with ketchup."

PART B. Using the answer line, complete each item below with the correct word from the box.

f. **attitude**	g. **contrast**	h. **excessive**
i. **fragile**	j. **indicate**	

_____ 6. Do you think a profit of 100 percent is ___?

_____ 7. The thermometer ___s that it's 20 above, but the wind makes it feel much colder outside.

_____ 8. Jill's ___ shows how confident she is. She believes that if she tries hard enough, she can do anything she wants to.

_____ 9. When Aunt Flora moved, she took her tea cup collection with her in the car because it was too ___ to put in the moving van with all the big, heavy things.

_____ 10. My dad can't get over the ___ between school today and when he was a boy, when students called teachers "Sir" and "Ma'am" and stood up when they entered the room.

SCORE: (Number correct) _____ × 10 = _____ %

Name: _____

Mastery Test: *Chapter 3 (Fixing Up Furniture; Barbara's Date)*

PART A. Using the answer line, complete each item below with the correct word from the box.

a. **determine**	b. **dispose of**	c. **evident**
d. **preserve**	e. **restore**	

_____ 1. My mother ___s dried flowers by spraying them with hair spray.

___*determine*___ 2. You can ___ a tree's age by counting the number of rings in its trunk.

_____ 3. To ___ the painting to its original beauty, many layers of dirt will have to be removed.

___*evident*___ 4. It's ___ that Jon is allergic to cats—he gets red marks all over his face whenever a cat's around.

_____ 5. When my wife is out of town, I let the garbage build up in the kitchen and then ___ it all just before she returns.

PART B. Using the answer line, complete each item below with the correct word from the box.

f. **accompany**	g. **desperate**	h. **pursue**
i. **rejection**	j. **scarce**	

___*scarce*___ 6. If gold weren't so ___, it wouldn't be so valuable.

___*accompany*___ 7. The invitation says that I can ask a date to ___ me to the wedding.

_____ 8. A telephone salesperson must get used to customers' ___s of their offers.

___*desperate*___ 9. After eating a huge box of salty popcorn, I was ___ for a tall glass of water.

_____ 10. Roni wanted to ___ a show-business career, even though her parents warned her that she'd have a hard time making a living as an actress.

SCORE: (Number correct) _____ × 10 = _____ %

Mastery Test: *Chapter 4 (Salesman; Peace at Last)*

PART A. Using the answer line, complete each item below with the correct word from the box.

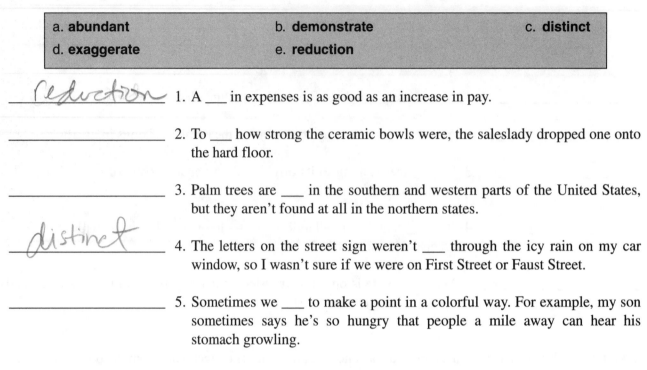

| a. **abundant** | b. **demonstrate** | c. **distinct** |
| d. **exaggerate** | e. **reduction** | |

reduction 1. A ___ in expenses is as good as an increase in pay.

_____ 2. To ___ how strong the ceramic bowls were, the saleslady dropped one onto the hard floor.

_____ 3. Palm trees are ___ in the southern and western parts of the United States, but they aren't found at all in the northern states.

distinct 4. The letters on the street sign weren't ___ through the icy rain on my car window, so I wasn't sure if we were on First Street or Faust Street.

_____ 5. Sometimes we ___ to make a point in a colorful way. For example, my son sometimes says he's so hungry that people a mile away can hear his stomach growling.

PART B. Using the answer line, complete each item below with the correct word from the box.

| f. **betray** | g. **comparison** | h. **dispute** |
| i. **inhabit** | j. **neutral** | |

dispute 6. My boyfriend and I have had a long-standing ___ over which is uglier, his purple tie or my spider earrings.

_____ 7. Golden eagles ___ nests that they build at the edge of cliffs.

neutral 8. In all the years my grandmother lived with us, she always remained ___ during her daughter and son-in-law's fights.

_____ 9. Ralph's mental illness makes it difficult for him to trust anyone. He feels that even his closest friends will someday ___ him.

comparison 10. A ___ of the ingredients in the expensive cake mix and the cheaper one showed there were very few differences between the two.

SCORE: (Number correct) _____ × 10 = _____ %

Name: _____

Mastery Test: *Chapter 5 (Study Skills; How to Control Children)*

PART A. Using the answer line, complete each item below with the correct word from the box.

a. aggravate	b. cease	c. humane
d. interference	e. obnoxious	

_____ 1. Lin took the phone off the hook so there would be no ___ while she worked on her taxes.

_____ 2. I don't find comics who insult people to be funny; instead, I think they're ___.

_____ 3. A ___ society will find a way to assist its handicapped citizens.

_____ 4. After being badly beaten in his run for mayor, William ___d to be involved in local politics.

_____ 5. Thomas's headache was ___d by the thought of having to lay off several workers in his department.

PART B. Using the answer line, complete each item below with the correct word from the box.

f. coincide	g. considerable	h. intentional
i. unstable	j. utilize	

_____ 6. The planter on the narrow patio railing may look ___, but actually, it's nailed down.

_____ 7. A typical apple tree loses a ___ amount of water each day—as much as twenty quarts.

_____ 8. Since my birthday and the last day of finals ___d, I had two reasons to celebrate on Friday.

_____ 9. My daughter was worried that I'd yell at her about the rip in her new coat, but I knew the tear was an accident, not ___.

_____ 10. For our art projects, my children and I ___ all sorts of materials that we'd otherwise throw away, such as magazine pictures, old wrapping paper, and shiny candy wrappers.

SCORE: (Number correct) _____ × 10 = _____ %

Mastery Test: *Chapter 6 (Toasters; A Mean Man)*

PART A. Using the answer line, complete each item below with the correct word from the box.

a. current	b. maintain	c. minimum
d. originate	e. reliable	

_____ 1. Karla is so ___ that her boss often leaves her in charge of the business.

_____ 2. Instead of quitting work, Ali will ___ his daytime job at the factory and take college classes at night.

_____ 3. The new store is so expensive that the ___ price there is for a simple-looking scarf that costs a hundred dollars.

_____ 4. The rumor that Iris was pregnant ___d when she was seen shopping for a stroller. In fact, she was shopping for her brother's baby.

_____ 5. My cousin is proof that people who don't understand their mistakes tend to repeat them. Her ___ husband is as violent as her last one.

PART B. Using the answer line, complete each item below with the correct word from the box.

f. advise	g. deprive	h. hesitate
i. objection	j. penalize	

_____ 6. Because jails are so full, some people are being ___d by being "jailed" in their own homes.

_____ 7. The President's ___ to the bill disappointed the many members of Congress who supported it.

_____ 8. The instructor ___d Lori to quit college and go to work until she was ready to study for her classes.

_____ 9. When the cashier asked for my phone number, I ___d. I wasn't sure I wanted a stranger to have our unlisted number.

_____ 10. My grandmother's early death ___d my mother of her youth because she had to bring up all her younger brothers and sisters herself.

SCORE: (Number correct) _____ × 10 = _____ %

Name: _____

Mastery Test: *Chapter 7 (Special Memory; Watch Your Manners)*

PART A. Using the answer line, complete each item below with the correct word from the box.

a. **astonish**	b. **consent**	c. **eager**
d. **horizontal**	e. **recollect**	

_____ 1. When the cats hear the sound of a can being opened, they run to the kitchen, ___ to be fed.

_____ 2. The Jensens' parrots ___ guests with their speaking ability—they can say hundreds of words and phrases.

_____ 3. I ___ my sister being born when I was four years old—it's my earliest memory.

_____ 4. If you were accused of a crime, would you ___ to taking a lie-detector test?

_____ 5. I scraped my car against the mailbox, leaving a ___ scratch that runs from the front tire to the back tire.

PART B. Using the answer line, complete each item below with the correct word from the box.

f. **abrupt**	g. **classify**	h. **complex**
i. **endure**	j. **exclaim**	

_____ 6. How would you ___ the movie you saw last night—as a comedy or an action-adventure?

_____ 7. Hal dislikes his brother-in-law so much that he can hardly ___ being in the same room with him.

_____ 8. A clown who was hiding behind a door jumped out unexpectedly. His ___ appearance made the children both scream and laugh.

_____ 9. As the child picked up the expensive crystal bowl, her mother ___ed, "Be careful with that!"

_____ 10. I bought a computer game for my nephew, but then exchanged it for something simpler—it was too ___ for a seven-year-old to figure out.

SCORE: (Number correct) _____ × 10 = _____ %

Name: _____

Mastery Test: *Chapter 8 (Brothers and Sisters; Kevin's First Date)*

PART A. Using the answer line, complete each item below with the correct word from the box.

a. **appeal**	b. **establish**	c. **potential**
d. **variety**	e. **wholesome**	

_____ 1. A group of single mothers have ___ed a babysitting-exchange club.

_____ 2. A ___ lifestyle includes plenty of time for exercise and relaxation.

_____ 3. The woman ___ed to the President to save her son from the death penalty.

_____ 4. Our supermarket has such a wide ___ of fruits that I don't even recognize them all.

_____ 5. Although Noreen usually gets C's in her classes, I believe she has the ___ to do much better work.

PART B. Using the answer line, complete each item below with the correct word from the box.

f. **adequate**	g. **awkward**	h. **customary**
i. **respond**	j. **vanish**	

_____ 6. It's often foggy here in the morning, but the fog will usually ___ by noon.

_____ 7. Jen never ___ed to my invitation to the Halloween party, so I'm not sure if she's coming or not.

_____ 8. In my family, it was ___ to measure us children on our birthdays, to see how much we had grown since the previous birthday.

_____ 9. My first meeting with Irene after our argument was ___ at first, but after a few minutes, I think we both felt more comfortable.

_____ 10. The staff meeting was moved to the larger front room because there wasn't ___ space for everyone in the old meeting room.

SCORE: (Number correct) _____ × 10 = _____ %	

Name: _____

Mastery Test: *Chapter 9 (Gym Program; Teaching a Lesson)*

PART A. Using the answer line, complete each item below with the correct word from the box.

a. **emphasis**	b. **interpret**	c. **propose**
d. **ultimate**	e. **vague**	

_____ 1. The ___ in my beginning art class is on drawing, not painting.

_____ 2. My brother thinks the ___ achievement in life is hitting a home run with the bases loaded and girls in the bleachers.

_____ 3. The president of the school board ___d that local businesses send workers to schools to teach students special skills.

_____ 4. I ___ed your comment that it was beautiful outside to mean it was sunny and warm, so I was surprised to see a skyful of falling snow.

_____ 5. The only direction Al gave me to his home was that it was on the same block as the firehouse. I thought he was being too ___ until I discovered there were no other homes on that block.

PART B. Using the answer line, complete each item below with the correct word from the box.

f. **brutal**	g. **discipline**	h. **eliminate**
i. **furthermore**	j. **resort**	

_____ 6. Some say that hypnosis can help people totally ___ bad habits.

_____ 7. Last year when I was out of work, I had to ___ to food stamps.

_____ 8. The robber took only ten dollars from Mrs. Turner, but his ___ attack put her in the hospital.

_____ 9. You can ___ your puppy to stop barking on command by firmly saying, "No!" and shaking a can containing several pennies.

_____ 10. Chimpanzees are very talented. They can learn to "talk" by using sign language. ___, some chimps have done "modern" paintings that have sold for hundreds of dollars.

SCORE: (Number correct) _____ × 10 = _____ %

Name: _____

Mastery Test: *Chapter 10 (Knowing How to Argue; A Change)*

PART A. Using the answer line, complete each item below with the correct word from the box.

a. **accustomed**	b. **misinterpret**	c. **occur**
d. **revise**	e. **version**	

_____ 1. Since all good writing is rewriting, it's important to ___.

_____ 2. The musical *West Side Story* is a modern-day ___ of *Romeo and Juliet*.

_____ 3. If you cut down the salt in your food gradually, you will become ___ to a low-salt diet.

_____ 4. When my children were young, I was so afraid that an accident would ___ that I purposely kept my kitchen knives very dull.

_____ 5. "Will you marry me?" Rita asked the minister, who ___ed the request and answered, "You're a wonderful woman, Rita, but I'm already married."

PART B. Using the answer line, complete each item below with the correct word from the box.

f. **anticipate**	g. **linger**	h. **miserable**
i. **reluctant**	j. **specific**	

_____ 6. I'm much more ___ when my baby is sick than when I myself am sick.

_____ 7. How long do you ___ it will take you to walk to work?

_____ 8. After the Aretha Franklin concert, some fans ___ed by the stage door, hoping to catch a glimpse of her.

_____ 9. Melissa was ___ to play the tuba because she didn't think that she wanted to carry such a large instrument home for practice.

_____ 10. I didn't want to leave anything to chance with the new babysitter, so I left ___ written instructions about supper, TV-watching, and bedtime.

SCORE: (Number correct) _____ × 10 = _____ %

Mastery Test: *Chapter 11 (Coma; The Office Doughnut Contest)*

PART A. Using the answer line, complete each item below with the correct word from the box.

a. **conscious**	b. **external**	c. **incredible**
d. **internal**	e. **remedy**	

_____ 1. Isn't it ___ that there are fish that can live on land?

_____ 2. When beans are boiled, their ___ layer may soften and come off.

_____ 3. As I was reading in the park, I became ___ of something large crawling on my neck.

_____ 4. Researchers are working on a ___ for people whose noses drip when they eat spicy foods.

_____ 5. People once believed that on the inside, Earth is hollow, but today's scientists say that the ___ part of the planet is made of hot iron.

PART B. Using the answer line, complete each item below with the correct word from the box.

f. **assume**	g. **exhaust**	h. **maximum**
i. **objective**	j. **protest**	

_____ 6. My parents' ___ in visiting me was to meet my new girlfriend.

_____ 7. Since the Rams are the best team, I ___ that they'll win the game.

_____ 8. Flying through several time zones can ___ people, leaving them with a tired feeling called "jet lag."

_____ 9. Nate wrote a letter to the president of the beer company to ___ the use of athletes in the company's television ads.

_____ 10. The ___ temperature ever officially recorded is 136 degrees Fahrenheit, in the city of El Azizia, Libya, on September 13, 1922.

SCORE: (Number correct) _____ × 10 = _____ %

Name: _____

Mastery Test: *Chapter 12 (People's Choice; Christmas Wars)*

PART A. Using the answer line, complete each item below with the correct word from the box.

a. **artificial**	b. **frequency**	c. **represent**
d. **temporary**	e. **triumph**	

_____ 1. I don't understand why the chicken is used to ___ a lack of courage.

_____ 2. Mario thinks that no one knows he's really bald. He doesn't realize how ___ his hairpiece looks.

_____ 3. The ___ of violent crimes in big cities is greater than in our small town, where such crime is rare.

_____ 4. No matter how many swimming tournaments he won, my brother was still thrilled over every new ___.

_____ 5. "Thank goodness our room-sharing is ___," Danielle told her sister. "I can't wait until your room is painted and you can move back in there."

PART B. Using the answer line, complete each item below with the correct word from the box.

f. **complicate**	g. **conscience**	h. **counsel**
i. **detect**	j. **transparent**	

_____ 6. I ___ed a slight flavor of cinnamon in the coffee.

_____ 7. Leon's ___ bothered him even when he killed a spider.

_____ 8. Mom ___ed me to consider working for a year after high school and then going on to college.

_____ 9. The man told the police officer that the money was a gift, but to the officer it was a ___ bribe.

_____ 10. Both my wife and I have to work Thursday evening, and, to ___ matters, none of our usual babysitters can watch the children then.

SCORE: (Number correct) _____ × 10 = _____ %

Name: _____

Mastery Test: *Chapter 13 (What's Your Type?; What a Circus)*

PART A. Using the answer line, complete each item below with the correct word from the box.

a. **intense**	b. **prosper**	c. **strive**
d. **tolerance**	e. **trait**	

_____ 1. Even though there are many other restaurants in the area, the little sandwich shop on the corner continues to ___ because of its great food, friendly service, and reasonable prices.

_____ 2. Our high school band is really excellent. The musicians ___ to be the very best they can.

_____ 3. The saying "Curiosity killed the cat" means that having ___ interest in things that don't concern you can lead you into trouble.

_____ 4. Some lizards have the odd ___ of changing color depending upon their surroundings.

_____ 5. When Suzanne picked out a plant for her south window, she realized she should choose one with a ___ for hot, sunny, dry conditions, such as a cactus.

PART B. Using the answer line, complete each item below with the correct word from the box.

f. **detract**	g. **foresight**	h. **interval**
i. **substance**	j. **withdraw**	

_____ 6. Although the school is only two years old, it is already too crowded—the planners should have had the ___ to make it larger.

_____ 7. Silly Putty is an amusing ___ that stretches, breaks, bounces, and copies pictures.

_____ 8. The poor performance of one of the actors ___ed from the quality of the play.

_____ 9. Even if you meet someone you'd rather ask to the dance, it would be very rude to ___ the invitation you've already given someone else.

_____ 10. I saw my cousin in July and again the next May. In that ___, she had grown three inches.

SCORE: (Number correct) _____ × 10 = _____ %

Mastery Test: *Chapter 14 (Kindness; The Stinking Rose)*

PART A. Using the answer line, complete each item below with the correct word from the box.

a. **consistent**	b. **evaluate**	c. **observe**
d. **phrase**	e. **random**	

_____ 1. If you ___ a magician closely, you can often see the tricks he plays to fool his audience.

_____ 2. "I don't care which goldfish you give me," said the woman to the pet-store clerk. "Just pick one out at ___."

_____ 3. Anita broke up with Raoul because he was not ___. One day he would say he wanted to be with her; the next he would say he needed more "space"; on the third he would say she was avoiding him.

_____ 4. A "tongue-twister" is a ___ like "rubber baby buggy bumpers" that is almost impossible to say quickly.

_____ 5. The police gathered all the facts they could. Now they will ___ them and decide if they have reason to make an arrest.

PART B. Using the answer line, complete each item below with the correct word from the box.

f. **approximately**	g. **cope**	h. **practical**
i. **significant**	j. **sole**	

_____ 6. The best way I know to ___ with a cold is to drink lots of hot liquids, stay warm, and have plenty of tissues on hand.

_____ 7. Working with a tutor has produced a ___ improvement in Rita's math grades.

_____ 8. The parents came up with a ___ way to have child care during their vacation: they invited a teenage friend along. She got a free vacation, and they got some free time.

_____ 9. Roger does not really care for Elaine. The ___ reason he is dating her is to make his former girlfriend jealous.

_____ 10. We never know exactly how many people will attend the family reunion, but it's usually ___ seven.

SCORE: (Number correct) _____ × 10 = _____ %

Name: _____

Mastery Test: *Chapter 15 (A Modern Fairy Tale; Wolf Children)*

PART A. Using the answer line, complete each item below with the correct word from the box.

a. **concept**	b. **confront**	c. **disrupt**
d. **eligible**	e. **harsh**	

_____ 1. The ___ that romantic love should be the reason for marriage is not accepted everywhere. In many cultures, people who barely know each other marry because their families believe they will make a good match.

_____ 2. In the famous story "The Bishop's Candlesticks," a good man receives a ___ punishment—seven years in prison!—for stealing a loaf of bread to feed his sister's starving family.

_____ 3. The shoplifter was ___ed by a store detective, who said, "I'd like to see what's in your pocket."

_____ 4. In order to be ___ for this contest, you must be between the ages of 11 and 13 and a resident of Montgomery County.

_____ 5. A swarm of angry bees ___ed the family's picnic, forcing everyone to run away and leave the food.

PART B. Using the answer line, complete each item below with the correct word from the box.

f. **authentic**	g. **characteristic**	h. **remote**
i. **shallow**	j. **thrive**	

_____ 6. When I am at the pet shop, I like to look at the saltwater tropical fish and admire their ___ bright colors.

_____ 7. The children's bedrooms are on the third floor of the house. They are so ___ that the kids can't hear their parents call from the first floor.

_____ 8. Businesses downtown used to ___, but since the mall opened outside of town, many have gone out of business and the others are struggling to survive.

_____ 9. "The bath is too ___," the little girl complained to her mother. "I want to pretend it's a swimming pool—can't you fill it up further?"

_____ 10. ___ Tiffany stained-glass lamps cost thousands of dollars, but there are many Tiffany-style copies that are beautiful and cost far less.

SCORE: (Number correct) _____ × 10 = _____ %

Mastery Test: *Chapter 16 (Mismatched Couple; Campaign)*

PART A. Using the answer line, complete each item below with the correct word from the box.

a. **burden**	b. **economical**	c. **extravagant**
d. **security**	e. **sympathize**	

_____ 1. Knowing that the local killer had finally been captured gave townspeople a welcome feeling of ___.

_____ 2. It's more ___ to spent a lot on cans of food when they're on sale than to buy only what you need each week.

_____ 3. Many single mothers have the ___ of supporting their family, caring for the children, and keeping up a home alone.

_____ 4. "I ___ with your difficulties in quitting smoking," the doctor said. "But if you don't quit, you're likely to suffer even more—you will ruin your health."

_____ 5. Although Mr. Jaimeson is very rich, he feels it would be ___ to spend all his money on luxuries when there are so many needy people in the world.

PART B. Using the answer line, complete each item below with the correct word from the box.

f. **apparent**	g. **automatic**	h. **fulfill**
i. **influence**	j. **transfer**	

_____ 6. In order to ___ all the conditions of my great-uncle's will, we had to find his parrot a home where she was allowed to fly freely during the daytime.

_____ 7. When Mr. Kennedy's boss wanted to ___ him to another city, he refused, saying his wife didn't want to leave her job.

_____ 8. Whoever is caught cheating in Geography gets an ___ F for the course.

_____ 9. Kurt's disappointment over not making the team was very ___. He had the expression of someone who had been run over by a truck.

_____ 10. As part of my effort to ___ my parents to let me have a New Year's party in our basement, I'm taking on extra responsibilities around the house.

SCORE: (Number correct) _____ × 10 = _____ %

Name: _____

Mastery Test: *Chapter 17 (The Famous Detective; Why So Quiet?)*

PART A. Using the answer line, complete each item below with the correct word from the box.

a. **appropriate**	b. **bewilder**	c. **emotion**
d. **investigate**	e. **legible**	

_____ 1. It turned out that the police officer who ___d drug crimes was an addict himself.

_____ 2. I never understood why people think it's not ___ to put one's elbows on the dinner table.

_____ 3. Since Clare's handwriting is barely ___, somebody else had better address the wedding invitations.

_____ 4. Undergoing surgery ___ed Dad. When he woke up, he didn't even know where he was or why.

_____ 5. Ernest tried to hide his ___s when he said goodbye to his parents, but there were tears in his eyes as he boarded the plane.

PART B. Using the answer line, complete each item below with the correct word from the box.

f. **communicate**	g. **deceive**	h. **earnest**
i. **fiction**	j. **theory**	

_____ 6. My parents know each other so well that they often ___ with only a glance or a smile.

_____ 7. In the library, ___ is organized alphabetically by the novelist's last name.

_____ 8. Many scientists accept the "Big Bang" ___, which states that the universe began with a huge explosion.

_____ 9. The sunny view outside my window ___d me into thinking it was warm outside. It's actually freezing cold out.

_____ 10. A girl at the subway station said she'd lost her purse and needed money to get home. She sounded so ___ that I gave her subway fare.

SCORE: (Number correct) _____ × 10 = _____ %

Name: _____

Mastery Test: *Chapter 18 (Fear of Speaking; Believe in Magic?)*

PART A. Using the answer line, complete each item below with the correct word from the box.

a. **distract**	b. **hostile**	c. **humiliate**
d. **impulse**	e. **timid**	

_____ 1. At his first dance, Zach hung around the back of the room, too ___ to ask anyone to dance.

_____ 2. "Stop tapping your pencil on the desk," the teacher warned a student. "The noise is ___ing everyone from their work."

_____ 3. It's hard enough to get up and speak in front of a friendly audience, but talking to a ___ audience takes real courage.

_____ 4. On an ___, Gina volunteered to host the office Christmas party. Once she got home, she said to her husband, "Why in the world did I do that? I don't have the time for all that extra work!"

_____ 5. The workers dislike their boss because he ___s them by scolding them angrily and calling them names in front of the whole factory.

PART B. Using the answer line, complete each item below with the correct word from the box.

f. **assure**	g. **crucial**	h. **extraordinary**
i. **perceive**	j. **revive**	

_____ 6. Gwen became alarmed when she ___d smoke pouring from a neighbor's window.

_____ 7. The children stared at the waitress, fascinated by her ___ fingernails—they were four inches long and painted bright purple.

_____ 8. The TV weather reporter ___d viewers that there would be beautiful weather for the weekend.

_____ 9. The high school sweethearts hadn't seen each other for thirty years, but a chance meeting ___d their romance, and they were soon married.

_____ 10. Loving touch is ___ to a baby. Without it, an infant does not develop well either physically or emotionally.

SCORE: (Number correct) _____ × 10 = _____ %

Name: _____

Mastery Test: *Chapter 19 (Miracle Runner; One of Those Days)*

PART A. Using the answer line, complete each item below with the correct word from the box.

a. **devote**	b. **dominate**	c. **idle**
d. **primary**	e. **overcome**	

_____ 1. The Harris twins, both six feet four inches and very athletic, ___ their high school basketball team.

_____ 2. Although the beauty shop offers manicures and facials, its ___ business is cutting and coloring hair.

_____ 3. Since their father had a stroke, the Martin brothers have ___d much of their time to caring for him.

_____ 4. A kind, understanding teacher helped Eliza ___ her fear of taking exams.

_____ 5. If you have so much homework to do, why are you sitting there ___ instead of working?

PART B. Using the answer line, complete each item below with the correct word from the box.

f. **abandon**	g. **alert**	h. **circumstances**
i. **function**	j. **theme**	

_____ 6. It was a struggle to stay ___ during the boring lecture.

_____ 7. Ms. Hendrix knows that many of her students live in difficult ___—for instance, one cares for his younger brothers while his mother is in the hospital, and another is working three jobs.

_____ 8. Will had to ___ his first idea for his science project, because he realized he did not have time to do the research.

_____ 9. One household appliance can serve several ___s. For example, a hair dryer can dry hair, dry fingernail polish, and dry damp clothing.

_____ 10. There are two important ___s running through the wonderful book *To Kill a Mockingbird*. One is the treatment of a black man falsely accused of a crime, and the other is a young boy and girl's relationship with a mysterious neighbor.

> ***SCORE:*** (Number correct) _____ × 10 = _____ %

Name: _____

Mastery Test: *Chapter 20 (Pregnancy and Alcohol; Criminal)*

PART A. Using the answer line, complete each item below with the correct word from the box.

a. **excerpt**	b. **exclude**	c. **hinder**
d. **misleading**	e. **severe**	

_____ 1. "If you're going to hand out party invitations at school, you must invite everyone in your class," the mother told her little boy. "It would be rude to ___ anyone."

_____ 2. When my roommate gets a letter from her boyfriend, she often reads me ___s from it.

_____ 3. Mark and Dorothy's "lovey-dovey" behavior in public is ___. In fact, they are thinking seriously about divorce.

_____ 4. A minor burn can be treated at home, but a ___ burn should always be seen by a doctor.

_____ 5. Tabitha's shyness ___s her from making friends easily.

PART B. Using the answer line, complete each item below with the correct word from the box.

f. **disregard**	g. **monotonous**	h. **obtain**
i. **prey**	j. **seize**	

_____ 6. "The Claw" is a coin-operated game in which the player tries to make the metal hand ___ a prize and drop it into a chute.

_____ 7. Ladybugs are valuable in a garden, because their ___ includes many insects that damage plants.

_____ 8. In order to ___ his father's permission to join the basketball team, Eric had to make all A's and B's in his classes.

_____ 9. "Pay no attention to that man behind the curtain!" The line is from a famous scene in *The Wizard of Oz*, in which the man pretending to be the wizard tells Dorothy and her friends to ___ what they have seen.

_____ 10. The ___ "clackety-clackety-clackety" sound of the train wheels soon caused most riders to fall asleep.

SCORE: (Number correct) _____ × 10 = _____ %

Name: _____

Mastery Test: *Chapter 21 (Traveling; Earth's Natural Supplies)*

PART A. Using the answer line, complete each item below with the correct word from the box.

a. **conflict**	b. **stress**	c. **unanimous**
d. **vary**	e. **vicinity**	

_____ 1. I never ___ my breakfast; every morning I eat oatmeal with raisins and chocolate chips.

_____ 2. Maybe it's no accident that in the ___ of the ski slopes, there's a place that rents crutches.

_____ 3. Political elections are never ___. A candidate who gets even 70 percent of the vote is doing very well.

_____ 4. An air traffic controller's job involves a lot of ___ because he or she is responsible for safe airplane landings.

_____ 5. Instead of yelling at each other when they had a serious ___ about something, my parents would stop talking to each other

PART B. Using the answer line, complete each item below with the correct word from the box.

f. **possess**	g. **procedure**	h. **renew**
i. **resources**	j. **sufficient**	

_____ 6. Even though there are only three people living in their house, the Smiths ___ five radios.

_____ 7. We wouldn't worry so much about our oil ___ if we made more use of solar energy.

_____ 8. The ___ for applying for a job usually involves filling out a form and then being interviewed.

_____ 9. Each year our country produces ___ trash to cover a twenty-four-lane highway from Los Angeles to Boston with a foot of garbage.

_____ 10. Although Meryl and Jay had gone steady in high school, they didn't see each other for many years. Then, after their twentieth high-school reunion, they ___ed their romance and got married.

SCORE: (Number correct) _____ × 10 = _____ %

Name: _____

Mastery Test: *Chapter 22 (More Fat, Anyone; Is Prison Effective?)*

PART A. Using the answer line, complete each item below with the correct word from the box.

a. **decay**	b. **expand**	c. **nevertheless**
d. **precise**	e. **vast**	

_____ 1. White furniture is difficult to keep clean; ___, that's what Jeannette wants in her living room.

_____ 2. Although we originally planned to have just eight people here for Thanksgiving dinner, the guest list has ___ed to fifteen.

_____ 3. When the beautiful old theater downtown began to ___, a group of townspeople formed a group to raise money and make it beautiful again.

_____ 4. Coming from a country where stores are small and selection is limited, Sergei was surprised by the ___ assortment of products in an American supermarket.

_____ 5. I don't know the ___ time that I was born. My parents just remember that it was in the early evening.

PART B. Using the answer line, complete each item below with the correct word from the box.

f. **abolish**	g. **corrupt**	h. **flexible**
i. **reform**	j. **tendency**	

_____ 6. The former mayor had a reputation for being ___. It was said that several crime organizations paid him to ignore their activities.

_____ 7. My ___ to speak first and think later has gotten me into trouble more than once.

_____ 8. No politician would be so foolish as to promise to ___ crime—while crime may be reduced, it can't be gotten rid of entirely.

_____ 9. Every year, my messy friend swears he will ___ and become a neat, organized person.

_____ 10. The children spent the morning playing with pipe cleaners, ___ fuzzy sticks that can be bent and twisted into any shape.

SCORE: (Number correct) _____ × 10 = _____ %

Mastery Test: *Chapter 23 (She Changed My Mind; So Sue Me)*

PART A. Using the answer line, complete each item below with the correct word from the box.

a. **clarify**	b. **extend**	c. **preconception**
d. **resemble**	e. **rigid**	

_____ 1. Because school was closed for so many snow days this winter, the school year will be ___ed for ten days.

_____ 2. A ruby and a garnet ___ each other in that both are red stones, but the ruby is more rare and more valuable.

_____ 3. I didn't understand the directions to Sue's house, so I asked her to ___ them.

_____ 4. People who meet the Queen are expected to follow a ___ set of rules. For example, they are not to speak to Her Majesty unless she speaks to them first.

_____ 5. Although many people have the ___ that a snake's skin is slimy, it is actually dry and cool.

PART B. Using the answer line, complete each item below with the correct word from the box.

f. **assert**	g. **evade**	h. **negligent**
i. **precaution**	j. **vertical**	

_____ 6. ___ fish owners who let the tank get dirty will soon have a tank full of dead fish.

_____ 7. The lazy boy ___s his chores by using every possible excuse, from "I've got homework!" to "I think I have a fever."

_____ 8. Because he sometimes gets carsick, Bud takes the ___ of taking medication before going on a long trip.

_____ 9. As part of a fitness test in gym class, students tried to climb up a ___ rope hanging from the ceiling to the floor.

_____ 10. Ever year, Grandmother ___s that she is going to retire from her job, but she never actually does it.

SCORE: (Number correct) _____ × 10 = _____ %

Name: _____

Mastery Test: *Chapter 24 (Public Speaking; Mrs. Thornton)*

PART A. Using the answer line, complete each item below with the correct word from the box.

a. **anxious**	b. **convince**	c. **inferior**
d. **overwhelm**	e. **thorough**	

_____ 1. Sam gets so ___ about shots that he'll faint before the needle even touches him.

_____ 2. If you keep up with class work, the final won't ___ you.

_____ 3. As far as flavor is concerned, store-bought mayonnaise is ___ to homemade mayonnaise.

_____ 4. Ms. Roberts' greedy nephew has ___d her that he's the only relative who truly cares about her and that she should leave all her money to him.

_____ 5. In the children's book *How the Grinch Stole Christmas,* the mean Grinch did a ___ job. He took away not only all the Christmas presents, but also all the Christmas trees and decorations.

PART B. Using the answer line, complete each item below with the correct word from the box.

f. **comprehend**	g. **dramatic**	h. **frank**
i. **illustrate**	j. **impression**	

_____ 6. To help gain the audience's attention, the lecturer wore ___ jewelry and brightly colored dresses.

_____ 7. The puzzled look on Vic's face showed he didn't ___ the algebra lesson.

_____ 8. To ___ for her students how to put a needle into a person's arm, the nursing teacher put one into a grapefruit.

_____ 9. Georgia found it hard to be ___ with her children about her past. She hated to admit she had used drugs as a teenager.

_____ 10. We left a lot of lights and a radio on when we went out of town so that thieves would have the ___ that someone was home.

SCORE: (Number correct) _____ × 10 = _____ %

Name: _____

Mastery Test: *Chapter 25 (Wacky Weddings; The Cost of Hatred)*

PART A. Using the answer line, complete each item below with the correct word from the box.

a. **commitment**	b. **formal**	c. **fundamental**
d. **precede**	e. **symbolize**	

_____ 1. I'd like to do something with you on Saturday, but I've made a ___ to babysit for my sister's kids.

_____ 2. When his classmates do something in alphabetical order, Aaron goes first, because his name ___s everyone else's.

_____ 3. Knitting isn't difficult once you learn the two ___ stitches: knit and purl.

_____ 4. A sign showing the letter P with a line through it ___s "No Parking."

_____ 5. The movie was about two wealthy people who were constantly going to ___ parties, he dressed in a tuxedo and she in a long evening dress.

PART B. Using the answer line, complete each item below with the correct word from the box.

f. **acquire**	g. **fragment**	h. **resent**
i. **solemn**	j. **spite**	

_____ 6. When the giant maple tree in our front yard was cut down, I saved a few ___s of wood as souvenirs.

_____ 7. Memorial Day is meant to be a ___ occasion, for it is the day we remember those who have lost their lives in war.

_____ 8. During her four years in college in Alabama, Sheree ___d a slight Southern accent.

_____ 9. Although the Robinsons are divorced, they do not treat each another with ___. They are still friendly and respectful to each other.

_____ 10. Many people in the community ___ the way that the new owners of the factory fired all the local workers and brought in new employees from out of town.

SCORE: (Number correct) _____ × 10 = _____ %

Chapter 1 (Johnny Appleseed; The Lovable Leech?)
1. a. challenge
2. c. peculiar
3. e. transform
4. b. fertile
5. d. surplus
6. j. suitable
7. h. principal
8. g. preference
9. f. dependent
10. i. solitary

Chapter 2 (Finding Fault; Hobbies)
1. b. category
2. e. frustration
3. a. analyze
4. d. deliberate
5. c. critical
6. h. excessive
7. j. indicate
8. f. attitude
9. i. fragile
10. g. contrast

Chapter 3 (Fixing Up Furniture; Barbara's Date)
1. d. preserve
2. a. determine
3. e. restore
4. c. evident
5. b. dispose of
6. j. scarce
7. f. accompany
8. i. rejection
9. g. desperate
10. h. pursue

Chapter 4 (Salesman; Peace at Last)
1. e. reduction
2. b. demonstrate
3. a. abundant
4. c. distinct
5. d. exaggerate
6. h. dispute
7. i. inhabit
8. j. neutral
9. f. betray
10. g. comparison

Chapter 5 (Study Skills; How to Control Children)
1. d. interference
2. e. obnoxious
3. c. humane
4. b. cease
5. a. aggravate
6. i. unstable
7. g. considerable
8. f. coincide
9. h. intentional
10. j. utilize

Chapter 6 (Toasters; A Mean Man)
1. e. reliable
2. b. maintain
3. c. minimum
4. d. originate
5. a. current
6. j. penalize
7. i. objection
8. f. advise
9. h. hesitate
10. g. deprive

Chapter 7 (Special Memory; Watch Your Language)
1. c. eager
2. a. astonish
3. e. recollect
4. b. consent
5. d. horizontal
6. g. classify
7. i. endure
8. f. abrupt
9. j. exclaim
10. h. complex

Chapter 8 (Brothers and Sisters; Kevin's First Date)
1. b. establish
2. e. wholesome
3. a. appeal
4. d. variety
5. c. potential
6. j. vanish
7. i. respond
8. h. customary
9. g. awkward
10. f. adequate

Chapter 9 (Gym Program; Teaching a Lesson)
1. a. emphasis
2. d. ultimate
3. c. propose
4. b. interpret
5. e. vague
6. h. eliminate
7. j. resort
8. f. brutal
9. g. discipline
10. i. Furthermore

Chapter 10 (Knowing How to Argue; A Change)
1. d. revise
2. e. version
3. a. accustomed
4. c. occur
5. b. misinterpret
6. h. miserable
7. f. anticipate
8. g. linger
9. i. reluctant
10. j. specific

Chapter 11 (Coma; The Office Doughnut Contest)
1. c. incredible
2. b. external
3. a. conscious
4. e. remedy
5. d. internal
6. i. objective
7. f. assume
8. g. exhaust
9. j. protest
10. h. maximum

Chapter 12 (People's Choice; Christmas Wars)
1. c. represent
2. a. artificial
3. b. frequency
4. e. triumph
5. d. temporary
6. i. detect
7. g. conscience
8. h. counsel
9. j. transparent
10. f. complicate

Chapter 13 (What's Your Type?; What a Circus)
1. b. prosper
2. c. strive
3. a. intense
4. e. trait
5. d. tolerance
6. g. foresight
7. i. substance
8. f. detract
9. j. withdraw
10. h. interval

Chapter 14 (Kindness; The Stinking Rose)
1. c. observe
2. e. random
3. a. consistent
4. d. phrase
5. b. evaluate
6. g. cope
7. i. significant
8. h. practical
9. j. sole
10. f. approximately

Chapter 15 (A Modern Fairy Tale; Wolf Children)
1. a. concept
2. e. harsh
3. b. confront
4. d. eligible
5. c. disrupt
6. g. characteristic
7. h. remote
8. j. thrive
9. i. shallow
10. f. Authentic

Chapter 16 (Mismatched Couple; Campaign)
1. d. security
2. b. economical
3. a. burden
4. e. sympathize
5. c. extravagant
6. h. fulfill
7. j. transfer
8. g. automatic
9. f. apparent
10. i. influence

Chapter 17 (The Famous Detective; Why So Quiet?)
1. d. investigate
2. a. appropriate
3. e. legible
4. b. bewilder
5. c. emotion
6. f. communicate
7. i. fiction
8. j. theory
9. g. deceive
10. h. earnest

Chapter 18 (Fear of Speaking; Believe in Magic?)
1. e. timid
2. a. distract
3. b. hostile
4. d. impulse
5. c. humiliate
6. i. perceive
7. h. extraordinary
8. f. assure
9. j. revive
10. g. crucial

Chapter 19 (Miracle Runner; One of Those Days)
1. b. dominate
2. d. primary
3. a. devote
4. e. overcome
5. c. idle
6. g. alert
7. h. circumstances
8. f. abandon
9. i. function
10. j. theme

Chapter 20 (Pregnancy and Alcohol; Criminal)
1. b. exclude
2. a. excerpt
3. d. misleading
4. e. severe
5. c. hinder
6. j. seize
7. i. prey
8. h. obtain
9. f. disregard
10. g. monotonous

Chapter 21 (Traveling; Earth's Natural Supplies)
1. d. vary
2. e. vicinity
3. c. unanimous
4. b. stress
5. a. conflict
6. f. possess
7. i. resources
8. g. procedure
9. j. sufficient
10. h. renew

Chapter 22 (More Fat, Anyone; Is Prison Effective?)
1. c. nevertheless
2. b. expand
3. a. decay
4. e. vast
5. d. precise
6. g. corrupt
7. j. tendency
8. f. abolish
9. i. reform
10. h. flexible

Chapter 23 (She Changed My Mind; So Sue Me)
1. b. extend
2. d. resemble
3. a. clarify
4. e. rigid
5. c. preconception
6. h. Negligent
7. g. evade
8. i. precaution
9. j. vertical
10. f. assert

Chapter 24 (Public Speaking; Mrs. Thornton)
1. a. anxious
2. d. overwhelm
3. c. inferior
4. b. convince
5. e. thorough
6. g. dramatic
7. f. comprehend
8. i. illustrate
9. h. frank
10. j. impression

Chapter 25 (Wacky Weddings; The Cost of Hatred)
1. a. commitment
2. d. precede
3. c. fundamental
4. e. symbolize
5. b. formal
6. g. fragment
7. i. solemn
8. f. acquire
9. j. spite
10. h. resent

Appendixes

This section contains the following:

1. **The Townsend Press Vocabulary Test (pages 141–146).** This 100-item diagnostic test contains 25 words from each of four TP vocabulary books:

   GROUNDWORK FOR A BETTER VOCABULARY, 2/e (recommended reading level 5–8)
   BUILDING VOCABULARY SKILLS, 2/e (recommended reading level 7–9)
   IMPROVING VOCABULARY SKILLS, 2/e (recommended reading level 9–11)
   ADVANCING VOCABULARY SKILLS, 2/e (recommended reading level 11–13)

   A student's score on this test (see page 146) will help determine which TP vocabulary book is appropriate for that student. The test, like the other materials in this manual, may be photo-copied for classroom use by instructors using any TP vocabulary book.

2. **Word Lists (pages 147–156).** Lists of the words taught in five TP vocabulary books—VOCABULARY BASICS as well as the four books listed above—are reprinted here for your convenience. Consulting these word lists may also help you determine which TP vocabulary book is best for your students.

NAME: _____

SECTION: _____ DATE: _____

Vocabulary Placement Test

SCORE: _____

This test contains 100 items. You have 30 minutes to take the test. In the space provided, write the letter of the choice that is closest in meaning to the **boldfaced** word.

Important: Keep in mind that this test is for placement purposes only. **If you do not know a word, leave the space blank rather than guess at it.**

_____ 1. to **deceive**   a) prove   b) mislead   c) reach   d) get back

_____ 2. **earnest**   a) serious and sincere   b) illegal   c) wealthy   d) hidden

_____ 3. **inferior**   a) not proper   b) clear   c) poor in quality   d) inside

_____ 4. to **comprehend**   a) describe   b) understand   c) make use of   d) prepare

_____ 5. **unanimous**   a) alone   b) animal-like   c) unfriendly   d) in full agreement

_____ 6. the **vicinity**   a) area nearby   b) city   c) enemy   d) information

_____ 7. **current**   a) healthy   b) modern   c) well-known   d) necessary

_____ 8. **internal**   a) forever   b) inside   c) outside   d) brief

_____ 9. **maximum**   a) least   b) expensive   c) cheap   d) greatest

_____ 10. an **objective**   a) goal   b) puzzle   c) cause   d) supply

_____ 11. a **potential**   a) favorite   b) possibility   c) refusal   d) desire

_____ 12. to **detect**   a) discover   b) make   c) follow   d) commit a crime

_____ 13. to **establish**   a) receive   b) delay   c) set up   d) attract

_____ 14. to **pursue**   a) follow   b) run from   c) suggest   d) create

_____ 15. **vague**   a) missing   b) unclear   c) kind   d) necessary

_____ 16. **suitable**   a) simple   b) needed   c) profitable   d) proper

_____ 17. a **category**   a) kindness   b) horror   c) type   d) question

_____ 18. **reluctant**   a) unwilling   b) lost   c) unhappy   d) well-known

_____ 19. to **coincide**   a) pay   b) decide   c) get in the way   d) happen together

_____ 20. to **inhabit**   a) enter   b) live in   c) get used to   d) understand

_____ 21. **apparent**   a) together   b) obvious   c) motherly   d) welcome

_____ 22. **accustomed**   a) in the habit   b) specially made   c) necessary   d) extra

_____ 23. to **revise**   a) give advice   b) go back   c) change   d) awaken

_____ 24. a **contrast**   a) purpose   b) choice   c) agreement   d) difference

_____ 25. **awkward**   a) forward   b) boring   c) clumsy   d) clever

(Continues on next page)

_____ 26. **urban**   **a)** of a city   **b)** circular   **c)** not allowed   **d)** large

_____ 27. **lenient**   **a)** light   **b)** not strict   **c)** delayed   **d)** not biased

_____ 28. to **endorse**   **a)** suggest   **b)** stop   **c)** support   **d)** start

_____ 29. a **novice**   **a)** book   **b)** false impression   **c)** beginner   **d)** servant

_____ 30. to **deter**   **a)** prevent   **b)** make last longer   **c)** refuse   **d)** damage

_____ 31. to **verify**   **a)** imagine   **b)** prove   **c)** keep going   **d)** cancel

_____ 32. **moderate**   **a)** generous   **b)** not final   **c)** medium   **d)** bright

_____ 33. a **diversity**   **a)** separation   **b)** conclusion   **c)** enthusiasm   **d)** variety

_____ 34. **accessible**   **a)** easily reached   **b)** itchy   **c)** difficult   **d)** folded

_____ 35. **lethal**   **a)** sweet-smelling   **b)** ancient   **c)** deadly   **d)** healthy

_____ 36. **vivid**   **a)** brightly colored   **b)** local   **c)** large   **d)** very talkative

_____ 37. to **convey**   **a)** allow   **b)** communicate   **c)** invent   **d)** approve

_____ 38. **inevitable**   **a)** unavoidable   **b)** dangerous   **c)** spiteful   **d)** doubtful

_____ 39. a **ritual**   **a)** business deal   **b)** war   **c)** ceremony   **d)** show

_____ 40. **elaborate**   **a)** large   **b)** complex   **c)** expensive   **d)** boring

_____ 41. the **essence**   **a)** fundamental characteristic   **b)** tiny part   **c)** much later   **d)** rule

_____ 42. to **coerce**   **a)** attract   **b)** refuse   **c)** remove   **d)** force

_____ 43. **skeptical**   **a)** stubborn   **b)** forceful   **c)** generous   **d)** doubting

_____ 44. **vital**   **a)** weak   **b)** stiff   **c)** necessary   **d)** unimportant

_____ 45. **innate**   **a)** learned   **b)** underneath   **c)** inborn   **d)** clever

_____ 46. a **vocation**   **a)** hobby   **b)** trip   **c)** report   **d)** profession

_____ 47. to **defy**   **a)** send for   **b)** resist   **c)** improve   **d)** approve

_____ 48. **adverse**   **a)** strict   **b)** profitable   **c)** rhyming   **d)** harmful

_____ 49. **consecutive**   **a)** late   **b)** following one after another   **c)** able   **d)** at the same time

_____ 50. **audible**   **a)** able to be heard   **b)** believable   **c)** willing   **d)** nearby

(Continues on next page)

_____ 51. to **encounter**   a) come upon   b) count up   c) depart from   d) attack

_____ 52. **obsolete**   a) modern   b) difficult to believe   c) out-of-date   d) not sold

_____ 53. to **terminate**   a) stop   b) continue   c) begin   d) approach

_____ 54. **altruistic**   a) honest   b) lying   c) proud   d) unselfish

_____ 55. to **enhance**   a) reject   b) get   c) improve   d) free

_____ 56. **nocturnal**   a) supposed   b) not logical   c) complex   d) active at night

_____ 57. to **suffice**   a) think up   b) be good enough   c) allow   d) reject

_____ 58. to **retaliate**   a) repair   b) repeat   c) renew   d) pay back

_____ 59. to **incorporate**   a) combine   b) anger   c) separate   d) calm

_____ 60. an **incentive**   a) fear   b) pride   c) concern   d) encouragement

_____ 61. **covert**   a) distant   b) hidden   c) changed   d) adjusted

_____ 62. to **alleviate**   a) make anxious   b) depart   c) infect   d) relieve

_____ 63. to **aspire**   a) dislike   b) strongly desire   c) impress   d) respect

_____ 64. an **extrovert**   a) shy person   b) magnet   c) main point   d) outgoing person

_____ 65. **prone**   a) disliked   b) tending   c) active   d) rested

_____ 66. **ominous**   a) happy   b) threatening   c) depressed   d) friendly

_____ 67. **complacent**   a) workable   b) lazy   c) self-satisfied   d) healthy

_____ 68. a **consensus**   a) majority opinion   b) total   c) study   d) approval

_____ 69. to **condone**   a) forgive   b) represent   c) arrest   d) appoint

_____ 70. **deficient**   a) forgotten   b) lacking   c) complete   d) well-known

_____ 71. **fallible**   a) capable of error   b) complete   c) incomplete   d) simple

_____ 72. **pragmatic**   a) ordinary   b) slow   c) wise   d) practical

_____ 73. **avid**   a) bored   b) disliked   c) enthusiastic   d) plentiful

_____ 74. **explicit**   a) everyday   b) distant   c) permanent   d) stated exactly

_____ 75. **ambivalent**   a) unknown   b) having mixed feelings   c) temporary   d) able to be done

(Continues on next page)

____	76. **vicarious**	a) experienced indirectly	b) lively	c) inactive	d) occasional
____	77. **rudimentary**	a) rude	b) planned	c) partial	d) elementary
____	78. to **collaborate**	a) respect	b) work hard	c) work together	d) search
____	79. to **venerate**	a) protect	b) create	c) make unfriendly	d) respect
____	80. **inadvertent**	a) unintentional	b) not for sale	c) distant	d) near
____	81. **predisposed**	a) against	b) unwilling to speak	c) undecided	d) tending beforehand
____	82. **robust**	a) extremely careful	b) healthy and strong	c) tall	d) loyal
____	83. **sedentary**	a) sitting	b) excessive	c) harmless	d) repeated
____	84. **clandestine**	a) well-lit	b) secret	c) noble	d) harmless
____	85. **austere**	a) wealthy	b) complex	c) plain	d) far
____	86. **notorious**	a) too bold	b) written	c) known widely but unfavorably	
		d) lacking skill			
____	87. **lucid**	a) clear	b) generous in forgiving	c) careful	d) bold
____	88. to **encompass**	a) include	b) draw	c) separate	d) purchase
____	89. **meticulous**	a) broken-down	b) curious	c) careful and exact	d) irregular
____	90. **innocuous**	a) delightful	b) harmless	c) dangerous	d) disappointing
____	91. to **rejuvenate**	a) set free	b) grow	c) refresh	d) make easier
____	92. to **facilitate**	a) approve	b) make easier	c) serve	d) clear from blame
____	93. **proficient**	a) proud	b) wise	c) skilled	d) well-known
____	94. to **emanate**	a) go above	b) run through	c) go down	d) come forth
____	95. to **implement**	a) encourage	b) carry out	c) insult	d) prevent
____	96. to **fabricate**	a) misinterpret	b) put away	c) clothe	d) invent
____	97. to **emulate**	a) be tardy	b) misunderstand	c) imitate	d) prepare
____	98. a **prognosis**	a) hope	b) prediction	c) opposite	d) memory
____	99. a **tumult**	a) uproar	b) uncertainty	c) series	d) scolding
____	100. to **insinuate**	a) demand	b) state	c) deny	d) hint

STOP. This is the end of the test. If there is time remaining, you may go back and recheck your answers. When the time is up, hand in both your answer sheet and this test booklet to your instructor.

To the Instructor: Use these guidelines to match your students with the appropriate vocabulary book.				
Score	0-24	25-49	50-74	75-90
Recommended Book	GBV	BVS	IVS	AVS

ANSWER SHEET

1. _____	26. _____	51. _____	76. _____
2. _____	27. _____	52. _____	77. _____
3. _____	28. _____	53. _____	78. _____
4. _____	29. _____	54. _____	79. _____
5. _____	30. _____	55. _____	80. _____
6. _____	31. _____	56. _____	81. _____
7. _____	32. _____	57. _____	82. _____
8. _____	33. _____	58. _____	83. _____
9. _____	34. _____	59. _____	84. _____
10. _____	35. _____	60. _____	85. _____
11. _____	36. _____	61. _____	86. _____
12. _____	37. _____	62. _____	87. _____
13. _____	38. _____	63. _____	88. _____
14. _____	39. _____	64. _____	89. _____
15. _____	40. _____	65. _____	90. _____
16. _____	41. _____	66. _____	91. _____
17. _____	42. _____	67. _____	92. _____
18. _____	43. _____	68. _____	93. _____
19. _____	44. _____	69. _____	94. _____
20. _____	45. _____	70. _____	95. _____
21. _____	46. _____	71. _____	96. _____
22. _____	47. _____	72. _____	97. _____
23. _____	48. _____	73. _____	98. _____
24. _____	49. _____	74. _____	99. _____
25. _____	50. _____	75. _____	100. _____

ANSWER KEY

1. b	26. a	51. a	76. a
2. a	27. b	52. c	77. d
3. c	28. c	53. a	78. c
4. b	29. c	54. d	79. d
5. d	30. a	55. c	80. a
6. a	31. b	56. d	81. d
7. b	32. c	57. b	82. b
8. b	33. d	58. d	83. a
9. d	34. a	59. a	84. b
10. a	35. c	60. d	85. c
11. b	36. a	61. b	86. c
12. a	37. b	62. d	87. a
13. c	38. a	63. b	88. a
14. a	39. c	64. d	89. c
15. b	40. b	65. b	90. b
16. d	41. a	66. b	91. c
17. c	42. a	67. c	92. b
18. a	43. d	68. a	93. c
19. d	44. c	69. a	94. d
20. b	45. c	70. b	95. b
21. b	46. d	71. a	96. d
22. a	47. b	72. d	97. c
23. c	48. d	73. c	98. b
24. d	49. b	74. d	99. a
25. c	50. a	75. b	100. d

To the Instructor: Use these guidelines to match your students with the appropriate vocabulary book.

Score	0-24	25-49	50-74	75-90
Recommended Book	*GBV*	*BVS*	*IVS*	*AVS*

List of the 240 Words in VOCABULARY BASICS

Note: The number after each word refers to the page in the text on which the word first appears.

ability, 62
accuse, 26
achieve, 212
admire, 200
admit, 128
advance, 218
advice, 116
agreement, 8
alarm, 152
allow, 86
amazed, 104
appear, 206
approach, 74
arrange, 122
assist, 230
attack, 20
attempt, 224
attract, 206
available, 128
avoid, 68
aware, 56
benefit, 32
bold, 200
cancel, 8
capable, 80
careless, 80
cautious, 116
claim, 26
collapse, 152
comfortable, 86
comment, 200
common, 206
compete, 134
competent, 230
conceal, 206
conclusion, 20

condemn, 182
condition, 212
confident, 104
confusion, 158
consider, 218
constant, 56
contain, 134
continue, 122
contribute, 128
courteous, 224
create, 62
curious, 8
daily, 14
damage, 62
damp, 74
decrease, 158
defeat, 116
defect, 116
defend, 152
definite, 38
delay, 32
delicate, 218
depend, 134
detail, 176
develop, 200
devour, 56
disaster, 170
discover, 56
disgust, 110
dismiss, 110
distant, 158
distract, 86
distressed, 56
donate, 104
dull, 128
duty, 212

effective, 134
effort, 104
embarrassed, 26
embrace, 182
emerge, 158
emphasize, 32
encourage, 128
enemy, 230
enormous, 206
entertain, 14
envy, 134
event, 20
examine, 230
excess, 164
excuse, 68
exhaust, 212
expect, 200
experience, 14
experiment, 129
expert, 122
explore, 224
express, 182
fact, 8
failure, 62
familiar, 182
fascinate, 170
flaw, 230
flexible, 8
fortunate, 38
furious, 80
generous, 170
glance, 62
glare, 176
gradual, 135
grasp, 218
gratitude, 63

List of the 250 Words in
GROUNDWORK FOR A BETTER VOCABULARY

Note: The number after each word refers to the page in the text on which the word first appears.

Words and Word Parts in *BUILDING VOCABULARY SKILLS*

List of the 260 Vocabulary Words

Note: The number after each word refers to the page in the text on which the word first appears.

absurd, 58
accelerate, 164
accessible, 76
acknowledge, 8
acute, 54
adapt, 110
adhere, 58
adverse, 164
advocate, 164
affirm, 118
affluent, 58
agenda, 20
alienate, 58
alleged, 118
allude, 118
alter, 50
alternative, 8
ample, 50
anecdote, 8
anonymous, 54
antidote, 20
apathy, 20
apprehensive, 54
appropriate, 8
arrogant, 54
ascend, 148
assess, 58
audible, 164
avert, 8
awe, 76
bestow, 54
bland, 20
blunt, 50
candid, 8
chronic, 50
chronological, 50
cite, 76
coerce, 118
coherent, 164
comparable, 164
compatible, 76
compel, 8
compensate, 46
competent, 164
compile, 58
comply, 8
concede, 42
conceive, 46
concise, 8
confirm, 160
consecutive, 164
consequence, 126

conservative, 42
conspicuous, 164
contempt, 58
contrary, 42
controversy, 156
convey, 88
data, 152
deceptive, 160
deduction, 156
defect, 58
defer, 92
defy, 160
delete, 16
delusion, 88
denounce, 42
derive, 46
destiny, 126
detain, 126
deter, 42
deteriorate, 164
devise, 88
dialogue, 12
dimensions, 156
diminish, 126
disclose, 42
discriminate, 144
dismal, 144
dismay, 110
dispense, 144
disperse, 156
distort, 156
diversity, 46
doctrine, 58
dogmatic, 58
dominant, 156
donor, 54
drastic, 8
dubious, 80
ecstatic, 80
elaborate, 114
elapse, 84
elite, 118
emerge, 114
encounter, 80
endeavor, 92
endorse, 24
equate, 92
erode, 24
erratic, 12
essence, 118
evasive, 84
evolve, 80

exempt, 76
exile, 110
exotic, 114
extensive, 12
fallacy, 80
fictitious, 80
finite, 148
fluent, 84
forfeit, 12
fortify, 12
frugal, 114
futile, 84
gesture, 110
gruesome, 24
gullible, 80
harass, 84
hypocrite, 24
idealistic, 24
illuminate, 12
illusion, 24
immunity, 118
impact, 24
impair, 118
impartial, 16
imply, 24
impose, 92
impulsive, 114
indifferent, 114
indignant, 92
indulgent, 114
inept, 152
inevitable, 92
infer, 84
infinite, 148
inflict, 148
ingenious, 148
inhibit, 46
initiate, 148
innate, 152
integrity, 16
intervene, 152
isolate, 12
lament, 152
legitimate, 16
lenient, 16
lethal, 84
liable, 80
liberal, 114
literally, 148
lure, 148
malicious, 92
mania, 148

List of the 40 Word Parts

Words and Word Parts in *IMPROVING VOCABULARY SKILLS*

List of the 260 Vocabulary Words

Note: The number after each word refers to the page in the text on which the word first appears.

absolve, 8	conventional, 42	explicit, 164
abstain, 84	conversely, 88	exploit, 16
acclaim, 16	covert, 80	expulsion, 114
adamant, 8	credible, 118	extrovert, 88
adjacent, 16	cryptic, 152	facade, 110
affiliate, 84	cursory, 118	fallible, 156
agnostic, 84	curt, 12	falter, 126
alleviate, 80	curtail, 76	feasible, 148
allusion, 24	cynic, 80	feign, 148
aloof, 164	decipher, 50	fiscal, 148
altruistic, 24	default, 50	flagrant, 42
ambivalent, 164	deficient, 152	flaunt, 126
amiable, 8	deficit, 84	flippant, 92
amoral, 8	degenerate, 54	fluctuate, 42
animosity, 8	demise, 80	formulate, 156
antagonist, 8	demoralize, 12	frenzy, 126
appease, 24	depict, 152	furtive, 148
arbitrary, 24	deplete, 122	gape, 148
aspire, 84	designate, 118	garble, 58
assail, 24	deter, 20	gaunt, 58
attest, 46	detract, 114	genial, 156
attribute, 46	detrimental, 152	gist, 126
augment, 164	devastate, 76	glib, 110
averse, 114	deviate, 118	gloat, 58
avid, 160	devoid, 144	habitat, 156
banal, 24	digress, 76	hamper, 126
benefactor, 80	dilemma, 12	haughty, 110
benevolent, 84	diligent, 122	hypothetical, 50
benign, 110	discern, 46	immaculate, 58
bizarre, 126	disdain, 114	impasse, 92
blase, 110	dispatch, 46	implausible, 54
blatant, 58	dispel, 164	implication, 20
blight, 58	dissent, 84	implicit, 152
calamity, 42	diversion, 84	implore, 144
charisma, 88	divulge, 114	improvise, 118
commemorate, 122	dwindle, 160	incentive, 76
complacent, 122	eccentric, 8	inclination, 12
comprehensive, 42	elation, 114	incoherent, 54
comprise, 110	elicit, 16	incorporate, 76
concurrent, 50	empathy, 122	indispensable, 76
condescend, 110	encounter, 8	inequity, 20
condone, 148	endow, 114	infamous, 80
conducive, 126	engross, 16	infirmity, 20
confiscate, 50	enhance, 46	infringe, 20
congenial, 92	enigma, 46	infuriate, 144
consensus, 122	epitome, 8	inhibition, 152
constitute, 50	escalate, 16	innovation, 20
constrict, 156	esteem, 160	intercede, 54
contemplate, 148	euphemism, 24	interim, 118
contemporary, 88	evoke, 160	intermittent, 76
contend, 88	exemplify, 46	intimidate, 144
contrive, 58	exhaustive, 156	intricate, 54

List of the 40 Word Parts

Words and Word Parts in ADVANCING VOCABULARY SKILLS

List of the 260 Vocabulary Words

Note: The number after each word refers to the page in the text on which the word first appears.

List of the 40 Word Parts